ONE BODY, ONE SPIRIT

ONE BODY, ONE SPIRIT

BY

THOMAS CORBISHLEY, S.J.

FOREWORD BY
THE ARCHBISHOP OF CANTERBURY

THE FAITH PRESS
Leighton Buzzard, Beds, LU7 7NQ
MOREHOUSE-BARLOW CO. INC., NEW YORK, U.S.A.

PRINTED IN GREAT BRITAIN
in 11pt. Garamond type
BY THE FAITH PRESS LTD.
LEIGHTON BUZZARD

SBN 7164 0245 9

GRANT that all who share in the Body and Blood of
Christ
May be brought together in unity by the Holy Spirit
And become one Body, one Spirit in Christ.
—from the Roman Mass

ALMIGHTY and everliving God, we most heartily
thank thee for that thou dost vouchsafe to feed us,
who have duly received these holy mysteries, with the
spiritual food of the most precious Body and Blood of
thy Son, our Saviour Jesus Christ; . . . and that we
are very members incorporate in the mystical body of
thy Son, which is the blessed company of all faithful
people . . .
*—from the Communion Service in
the Book of Common Prayer*

CONTENTS

FOREWORD

by the Archbishop of Canterbury

For the first time the Archbishop of Canterbury's Lent Book is written by a Roman Catholic author, and I cannot doubt that it will have thousands of grateful readers who will find themselves helped forward along Christ's road of unity.

Taking the Eucharist as his main theme, Father Corbishley shows the inner unity which lies beneath our historic differences of understanding, and the way in which some of the differences are resolved if the right questions are asked and answered. I am sure that this book will immensely help the reconciling work to which the *Agreed Statement on the Eucharist* produced by the Anglican-Roman Catholic International Commission has already contributed so much.

But Father Corbishley's book is not only for the theologian and the ecumenical devotee. It will deepen any Christian's understanding of the mystery of Jesus Christ in relation to mankind and the world, and of the ways in which the Holy Sacrament is a key to His purpose for all human life. Whatever Church we belong to we ought to be better Christians if we follow Father Corbishley's guidance through the words and actions of our Lord in the Holy Scriptures.

✝ MICHAEL CANTUAR:

PREFATORY NOTE

It is the nature of the series to which this small volume is a contribution that they should promote devotion rather than learning, even if true devotion must be based on authentic learning. It has seemed undesirable therefore to introduce into the text references to works of scholarship or other notes. But, whilst the book is the outcome of a lifetime of reading, so that no comprehensive acknowledgement can possibly be made, two recent publications call for special mention. The suggestion on which the first section of Chapter II is based comes from a remarkable lecture by Professor David Daube, which deserves far more notice than it has received. Entitled *He That Cometh*, it was delivered at St. Paul's under the auspices of the London Diocesan Council for Christian-Jewish Understanding in October 1966. Those who wish to know more about the development of eucharistic belief, which could only be touched on briefly in Chapter IV, will find much help in *Eucharistic Theology Then and Now* (S.P.C.K.).

But above all what I wish to do here is to express my sense of profound gratitude to the Archbishop of Canterbury who has done me the honour of inviting me to write this book which goes forth under the banner of his renown. My fervent hope is that it will make some small contribution to the cause of Christian unity, to which he has so enthusiastically dedicated himself—an enthusiasm which I should wish to share in my own measure.

CHAPTER I

INTRODUCTORY: THE PROBLEM

'Men ought to take heed of rending God's Church by two kinds of controversies. The one is, when the matter of the point controverted is too small and light, not worth the heat and strife about it, kindled only by contradiction. . . . The other is, when the matter of the point controverted is great, but is driven to an over-great subtilty and obscurity. . . . A man that is of judgement and understanding shall sometimes hear ignorant men differ, and know well within himself that those which so differ mean one thing, and yet they themselves would never agree.' Francis Bacon, quoted in *The Royal Society: Concept and Creation* by Margery Purver, p. 148.

(i)

Lent is a time when the Church encourages us to turn our thoughts towards the central theme of all Christian living, the restoration of our fallen human nature to its integrity by the life-giving work of Christ. It is a phase in the liturgical year when all Christians, whatever their disagreement on this or that aspect of doctrine, worship, devotion or ecclesiastical structure, are at one in confessing their inadequacy, their need of grace, their acceptance of that grace from God through Christ. What Christian fails to admit the truth of Paul's words:

'All men have sinned and are deprived of the divine splendour, and all are justified by God's free grace alone, through his act of liberation in the person of

13

Jesus Christ. For God designed him to be the means of expiating sin by his sacrificial death, effective through faith' (Rom. 3: 23–4).

True as it is that a term like 'justified' has been the occasion for bitter theological wrangles, the essential meaning of that passage is something which no Christian would reject. At the foot of the Cross all our quarrels are forgotten. Yet there is one element which is central to each and every form of Christian belief and practice that accepts any form of sacramental theology, about which some of the most passionate disputations and even the most savage persecutions have arisen. That element is, of course, the Holy Eucharist, recognised by us all as the means *par excellence* by which the members of the Church are most effectively brought into relationship with the saving work of Christ on Calvary.

The precise nature and what we may call the mechanism of that relationship have long been in dispute. It is the chief concern of this book to take a fresh look at the problems raised by that relationship, in the hope that even to be reminded of the fact of such a link, however it is to be explained, will help us all to a closer sense of fellowship in face of a commonly shared mystery. For it is surely because we have either misunderstood or, it may be, have lost sight of this abiding fact that what was originally given to His Church by Jesus as both symbol and effective means of unity should, in effect, have become such a rock of offence. The more we can deepen our consciousness of the meaningfulness of Christ's work in us and for us, in and through the mystery of His Body, broken for us, His Blood, shed for us, the more shall we long for the day when, in true unity of heart and mind, we shall joyously and in full Christian love approach the one altar, to share together that which is the common spiritual food and drink of all Christian men and women, the ever-present reality of the Word that was made human flesh, in order that He might truly be with us to the end of time.

We begin then by reminding ourselves that we are dealing with a mystery, that is to say with a process that takes place radically in the world of God's action upon us, though the fact that that action does have its effect in us and in our world means that there are aspects of it which we can and should investigate. For the very doctrine of the Incarnation means that we can touch the intangible, see the invisible, know the unknowable. This paradox at the very heart of our faith is at once an encouragement and a warning—an encouragement to apply our human minds to the human aspect of that divine action, a reminder that, since we are also handling divine things, our minds will never be adequate to their comprehension.

(ii)

There are few signs of friendship more important than an invitation to a meal. Not all such invitations, it is true, are necessarily indications of friendship. The calculated hospitality of the business-man, entertaining his clients at the taxpayer's expense, or the scarcely less scheming diplomacy of the society hostess, are not friendly occasions, except in the most superficial sense. But, where true friendship is present, the dinner-party or the buffet-supper are occasions that both manifest and deepen those bonds of affection which are so precious in the range of our human relationships. So it is only to be expected that in the area of man's religious experience the idea of a sacred meal should have been common. In the Graeco-Roman tradition, for example, the *lectisternium,* in which a banquet was prepared for the gods themselves, manifested a desire for a friendly relationship with the divine powers which it was felt could be achieved by having them to a meal.

Central to the Jewish tradition, existing it would seem long before the Temple was planned, is the Seder, the Passover meal, which, whatever its origins may have been, came to be accepted as a commemoration of the great deliverance from the Egyptian captivity. Before the destruction of the Second Temple, its ritual was directly associated, through the eating of the Lamb, with the sacrificial liturgy celebrated in Jerusalem. Since A.D. 70 it has continued to commemorate those centuries when, like Mecca for the Moslem, Jerusalem was the focal point of all Jewish religious activity. But the Passover meal has always been more than an exercise in nostalgia. It looked back to the great deliverance from Pharaoh; it looked forward to the final triumph of Israel in the coming Messianic age. It is perhaps the most powerful of all the forces which have gone to develop and maintain the astonishing solidarity of the Jewish people.

It is, as we know, out of this very heart and core of the ancient religion of Israel that the Christian eucharistic service took its rise. At the Last Supper the Holy Communion was instituted. Indeed, it is true to say that the Last Supper was the First Holy Communion. For Christians, the abiding hope of the great Jewish family, ever renewed, ever symbolised in the Passover Haggadah, was finally realised. In their Messianic hope, all Jews, whatever their internal divisions, are firmly united. Can we say the same of all Christians? Is it not necessary to admit, with sorrow, that what was appointed by Christ to be the effective sign of our oneness in Him has become, in effect, one of the major causes of our disunity? The 'one loaf', symbolising the Body of all Christian believers, has been broken, not to be shared out to all but to be a fragmented and, in every sense of the word, scandalous expression of our mutual suspicion and intolerance. It is as though we had to say, in answer to Paul's challenging question : 'Is Christ divided?', 'Alas, yes'.

It is the argument of this book that, if we are to overcome our divisions and, in that authentic, divine unity for which Christ prayed, gather up the broken fragments to reconstitute the 'one loaf' of our common belief, we must return to our origins and study both the way in which Christ fulfilled the Old Covenant and also the profound and wide-ranging implications of that fulfilment. Week after week, Roman Catholics, Orthodox Christians of every rite, Anglicans and followers of every shade of Reformed belief and practice, recite substantially the same words, as they celebrate their various liturgies. They are at one in recognising that, somehow, this communion rite is related to, expresses, emphasises, represents, recalls, embodies the saving work of Christ on the Cross. Yet, down the centuries, men and women have been put to death, families have been rent apart, Christians have become totally un-Christian in their behaviour one to another, and all because they held that *their* understanding of this mystery was the only authentic one. They are at one in accepting the basic truth that, in that saving work, lies their hope in this world and in the world to come. When it comes to explaining or describing the nature or process of this work, prejudices emerge. The issue is literally prejudged in the light of some traditional explanation, some familiar phraseology. If it is suggested that perhaps the phraseology needs to be looked at again to make sure that it still expresses the truth it was originally intended to convey, intemperate charges of heresy, modernism, scepticism are thrown about as though the enquirer was trying to eviscerate the abiding truth and not merely seeking to make its expression more meaningful and, therefore, more effective for the life of the believer.

What we all need to learn is that what are called the 'conservative' and the 'liberal' or 'progressive' approaches to theological truth have, in themselves, nothing whatsoever to do with religion. They are simply manifestations of differing psychological attitudes which may get attached to scientific, artistic, economic or political questions just as much as to matters of theology. Theology is, after all, no more than the name we give to man's attempts to put into words certain truths which, by definition, are and always will be beyond man's capacity to understand and, *a fortiori,* to put into words. This is not to say that words do not matter. Since religion is, in one department, a matter of community it calls

17

B

for some possibility of communication. Whilst our growing appreciation of religious truth depends ultimately on the work of the Spirit of God in the soul, the Spirit does make use of human agencies. Hence the theologian has an important responsibility. But his responsibility is to the truth itself and not to any system or code or linguistic formula as such, however time-honoured, even at times essential, these things may be. Clearly, his responsibility to the truth is related to his duty to clarify and communicate that truth. In view of the basic conservatism which most human beings manifest in their approach to their deepest concerns, he will always seek to be tender in his dealings with those he is hoping to enlighten, to lead into a fuller awareness of the truth.

At the same time, he will be encouraged by the example of Christ himself, who, in the end, went to His death because He was for ever trying to bring out the deeper truth implicit in traditional language. For Christ's attempt set Him on a collision course, heading for a clash with those who, for whatever reason, saw the truth of God and the effectiveness of God's action exclusively in terms of certain accepted forms, whether of language or ways of behaving. It is, in the end, the *truth* that makes us free. Paul, again, for all his insistence on the need to preserve the purity of the Gospel teaching, recognised also that the 'milk' of an earlier teaching might need to be replaced with the 'strong meat' of a more adult presentation of the faith. Fidelity is not synonymous with stagnation.

These general remarks about the nature of theological dialogue have a particular relevance in the context of eucharistic doctrine. Terms like 'transubstantiation', 'consubstantiation', 'impanation', 'sacrifice', 'memorial', and so on have become shibboleths to distinguish the various schools of theological interpretation. Yet they are only valuable in a genuinely religious way if they really do illuminate a truth which is in grave danger of being obscured by the dust of sectarian conflict. In most Christian traditions, the command 'Lift up your hearts' precedes the introduction of the narrative of Institution. The command is scarcely less relevant to any discussion of eucharistic doctrine. We need to lift up our minds and hearts above the debates of the past, to try to recognise Christ in the 'breaking of bread', to see, in so far as we can, what He intended to achieve in giving us this great Gift, what role it plays in the whole Christian understanding of God's purposes. And, whilst it may be of value to try to see how Christians became divided over this issue, such an investigation will help our purpose only if it is conducted in a spirit not of controversial acrimony but out of a sympathetic effort to enter into the minds of those with whom we may happen to disagree but whose very attempt to provide an alternative formulation may shed light on the crucial issue.

CHAPTER II

FROM PASSOVER TO EUCHARIST

'You shall keep this day as a day of remembrance and make it a pilgrimage feast, a festival of the Lord; you shall keep it generation after generation, as a rule for all time. . . . You shall observe these commandments because this was the very day on which I brought you out of Egypt.' Exodus 12 : 14, 17.

'The corn itself is in its far-off way an imitation of the supernatural reality; the thing dying, and coming to life again, descending and re-ascending beyond all nature. The principle is there in nature because it was first there in God himself. Thus one is getting in behind the nature religions, and behind nature to Someone who is not explained by, but explains, not, indeed, the nature religions directly, but that whole characteristic behaviour of nature on which nature religions were based.' C. S. Lewis, *Undeceptions,* pp. 59–60.

(i)

When we read the accounts of the Last Supper and the apparently abrupt way in which our Lord, with no sort of preliminary, took the bread and declared it to be His body, giving it to His disciples to eat, familiarity has prevented us from being surprised. For us, the significance of this happening has become an accepted part of our religious observance.

Puzzled as we may be by the immense problems raised by the presence of Christ in the consecrated elements, wherever they may be, we are yet not otherwise taken aback by what the evangelists have described. But how was it with the apostles? When their Master foretold His coming betrayal by one of them, they were full of questions. When He spoke of His imminent departure and return, when He spoke of their seeing the Father, Philip immediately asked to be shown the Father. But when Christ made this staggering pronouncement—'This, this piece of unleavened bread, is my Body'—they apparently accepted His words without demur. Had there been any sort of preparation, anything leading up to this astonishing idea?

Of course, there had been the remote preparation outlined in the sixth chapter of the fourth gospel, the great eucharistic discourse, in which He had promised to give himself, His flesh, for the life of the world. But all that had been in Galilee, possibly as much as twelve months ago. Had there been nothing else, no other sort of more direct and immediate warning, no hint or indication of what He was now about to do? True as it may well be that the Synoptic accounts of what had occurred in the upper room reflect the faith and practice of the first generation of Christians who, within a quarter of a century, were already accustomed to the idea of Christ's presence in the eucharistic species, this in no way explains how that faith and practice had come to be. How was it possible for the apostles themselves, beset as they were with every sort of doubt and uncertainty, nevertheless to be able, as it would seem, to take in their stride, as something almost natural, almost inevitable, this fantastic suggestion?

To explain their willingness to accept so easily something which, taken by itself, seems so utterly outside the realm of normal religious life, we shall need to look a little more closely at the detail of the context in which the words of institution were first uttered. We know, to begin with, that the Passover festival commemorated the great mercies which God had shown to His chosen people. We know that its whole spirit was to express the gratitude of the people for their deliverance from slavery. We know from contemporary literature that, during the lifetime of Christ, there was widespread expectation that the promised Messiah would shortly appear. As the centuries have passed, the expectation of a human deliverer has receded more and more from the thought of the Jewish people. It is difficult to believe that, in the days of Christ, that expectation would not somehow be embodied in the Passover liturgy, even if it has disappeared completely from modern forms of that worship.

Or has it? For it has been suggested of late that there survives even to this day a fragment, a detail which demands a messianic explanation. At the beginning of the celebration, after calling upon the name of God, creator of the fruit of the vine, of the fruits of the earth, the assembled company begins the feast by drinking a cup of wine and eating some green vegetable, as a kind of *hors d'oeuvre*. The host or president, who has before him three pieces of unleavened bread, breaks off a large portion from the middle one of the three, wraps it in a napkin and conceals it.

The name of the portion thus broken off and hidden is *Afikoman*. It is universally recognised that this is not a Hebrew or Aramaic form, and is quite certainly of Greek origin. Since the *Afikoman* is to be 'discovered' and eaten at the end of the meal, Jewish scholars have suggested that it means something like 'dessert'. It was to be that strange interpreter, Robert Eisler, who half a century ago hit upon what must surely be the correct meaning. Eisler's advocacy unfortunately was not such as to commend its general acceptance. It has been left to a much more sober and not less learned commentator to revive the idea. David Daube, an orthodox Jew with a vast knowledge of Rabbinic Judaism, has this to say: '*Aphiqoman* is the Greek *aphikomenos* or *ephikomenos*, "The Coming One", "He that Cometh", Hebrew *habba*, Aramaic *'athe*. But for the theological and historical consequences that follow, it is hard to believe that this obvious, philologically easiest, *naheliegendste* derivation would have been overlooked in favour of the most far-fetched and tortuous ones . . .'

Such a meaning for the *Afikoman* sheds a flood of light on the story of the institution of the eucharist, sketchy as are the surviving details of that story. A modern Jewish description of the Passover liturgy speaks as follows:

Since the meal cannot be ritually complete without eating the *Afikoman*, the leader or host now calls for it. . . . The *Afikoman* is our substitute for the Paschal Lamb, which in days of old was the final food of the Seder feast. Each person is given a portion which is eaten in a reclining position.

Picture, then, the Leader, at the Last Supper, calling for the *Afikoman*, which, we remember, has been hidden since the beginning of the proceedings, and saying to His followers: 'The *Afikoman*, He who Comes, who was hitherto hidden, has now come. This piece of bread is indeed my very self, no longer in type but in reality. When, therefore, you eat it, you are eating no longer a symbol, a foreshadowing of a future reality. You are eating my very self. Whenever, in days to come, you eat this same *Afikoman*, remember that I am truly present in it and therefore in you.'

The meal proper is now over, but there follow a number of prayers, from which one or two significant passages may be quoted. Whilst we cannot, of course, be certain that these date back to the time of Christ, the ideas they embody seem so apposite that no Christian can fail to find in them a striking parallel with his own thoughts. Thus, after grace is said, one prayer contains this striking phrase:

We thank thee for thy covenant sealed in our flesh,

a reference, of course, to circumcision, yet finding a more complete fulfilment in the flesh of Christ's circumcised body, soon to be broken to bring into being the new covenant.

Shortly, too, the company prays:

Hasten the Messianic era

and again

May the merciful father find us worthy of the messianic era.

Almost immediately, with the prayer

> Blessed art thou, O Lord our God, king of the Universe
> who createst the fruit of the vine

the company drinks the third of the four cups of wine which
by tradition are drunk during the Passover feast.

It is, then, against such a background that we can re-read
Luke's account:

> 'I have longed to share this paschal meal with you before
> my passion; I tell you I shall not eat it again, till it finds
> its fulfilment in the kingdom of God. And he took a
> cup, and blessed it and said: Take this and share it
> among you; I tell you, I shall not drink of the fruit of
> the vine again, till the kingdom of God has come.'

All this is clearly preliminary to the meal itself, although both
Matthew and Mark introduce the second part of the saying
after the account of the institution of the holy eucharist. We
must surely see it as part of that immediate preparation of the
minds of the apostles which was surely necessary if they were
to accept the reality of what was shortly to be done.

Daube, in the lecture from which I have already quoted,
sums up the argument thus:

> 'We are so used to Jesus's action on that occasion that
> we no longer wonder about its peculiar character, take it
> as, in the circumstances, the most natural thing in the
> world. A moment's reflection, however, will expose the
> untenability of this attitude. Let me put it this way: had
> no ritual of the kind preserved in the Jewish Passover
> eve service existed, and had Jesus suddenly distributed
> a cake of unleavened bread and said of it, "This is my
> body", His disciples, to put it mildly, would have been
> perplexed. With such a ritual referring to "The Coming
> One" in existence, the self-revelation made sense. Up to
> then, the fragment of unleavened bread was, so to
> speak, the Messiah in the abstract, the unknown
> Messiah; now He was known. The ritual of eating "The
> Coming One" . . . must precede the institution of the

Eucharist, the decisive point of which was the identification : the ancient expectation was now fulfilled. If we did not find such a ritual in the Jewish background, we should have to invent it. As it does occur, the reasonable course seems to be to accept it for what it is.'

Not that the foregoing suggestion puts an end to all our problems. What it does is at least to enable us to see how appropriate it would have been for Jesus to behave in this particular way, to institute precisely this memorial of himself, to round off and complete the long history of His people in a manner which, without doing violence to anything that had gone before, would deepen and enrich its whole meaning.

(ii)

But there are yet more profound considerations to be introduced if we are to enter more successfully into the mind of Christ. Daringly, yet, it would seem, not impertinently we must allow ourselves to speculate about the whole development of His thought until this moment. Perhaps we can begin with that incident in His life when, at the age of twelve, He was found in the Temple, amazing the scholars there with the maturity of His mind. The year is probably A.D. 6, when Archelaus was deposed by Augustus, and his tetrarchy taken over as a Roman province. It was a year of seething revolt, a year when a sort of holy war was proclaimed against Rome by a Galilean, a man from the region so familiar to Jesus himself.

It was hardly likely that the discussion turned on abstract questions of theology, on the niceties of canon law, on points of ecclesiastical etiquette. For the first time in His young life, Jesus was confronted with the agonising problem of His own destiny. He had grown up in a circle which—if we are to take the Infancy narratives as in any way embodying facts— accepted Him as the future saviour of His people. He could not but be aware of this expectation. Yet what could it mean, in practice? The city was in a turmoil, some maintaining that the only course was to accept the Emperor's decision, others hoping, secretly or openly, that the revolt of Judas and his followers would succeed. What was to be His role in all this?

For the present, at any rate, He realised that His only course was to return to Nazareth with His parents, and remain there, an obedient son, preparing himself for whatever might be. Inevitably, His reading of the scriptures would have for Him a meaning, a personal application which they have had for no other human being. The whole thrust of the divine promises pointed towards himself as the one who was to come, the anointed one, the king of glory, seated at the right hand of God, the son of David, Son of Man; the servant, too, meek, compassionate, yet set to judge the nations; suffering servant, bearing the sorrows of the world, carrying upon His shoulders the burden of the world's sin and thereby healing the wounds of mankind. Though He advanced in 'wisdom', He could never completely comprehend the full implications of His destiny, so manifold, so complex, so paradoxical. All He could do was to submit himself to the immediate task as it presented itself, waiting for the Father's will to disclose itself at the appointed time. It was through the Baptist's call to national repentance that the summons came. Since He bore His people's sin, it was fitting that He should present himself to be baptised, as a sign of His repentance for their sin, and, at the same time, as an anticipation of that baptism of blood which would be His final act of redemptive satisfaction. Now that the summons had come, He felt the urge to prepare himself more directly for what lay ahead. Hence His retirement into the wilderness of Judaea, that well-known region to which men retired to make their souls, to meditate upon the meaning of God's call to His people, to speculate about their own contribution to the spiritual and social well-being of the nation.

It was there, in what we think of a series of 'temptations', that He gained a clearer insight into the meaning of Messiahship. Specifically in the vision of the glory of the kingdoms of this world did He come to see beyond possibility of doubt that the messianic kingdom was not that sort of thing. For to acquire an earthly kingdom meant, inevitably, some sort of compromise with the standards on which political power is based. The striving for the coming of the Kingdom of God was paramount. To that every sort of earthly concern must be subordinated. Yet the recognition of this truth meant, as He knew only too well, that He would find enemies all about Him—on the one hand, the sceptical and worldly Sadducees, who represented the most powerful element in the priestly caste, and who subordinated their spiritual principles to the political necessities of the situation in which survival meant collaboration with the occupying pagan power; on the other the fanatical party of Zealots who saw violence as the only hope for national liberation.

In between was the numerous party of the Pharisees, some of whom certainly sympathised with the aims of the Zealots, though as a class they looked for salvation to a meticulous observance of the Law. Yet this would not do either, since the letter of the Law so easily defeated its whole purpose, the expression of a loving worship of a God seen to be loving.

Inevitably, then, in choosing to associate himself with none of the existing parties, He committed himself to a life of lonely idealism, an idealism untainted by worldliness, violence or unspiritual legalism. In so committing himself He was, as He well knew, committing himself to a way which would lead through misunderstanding and rejection to final ostracism and death. Yet only so could He bring about the redemption of His people from the various forces of evil that threatened their integrity as the chosen people of God. He was entering on the path that had been followed by all the prophets who had encountered hatred, physical danger and often death.

All He could hope to do in the time that was left to Him was to collect a group of followers who might be educated to see the truth as He saw it, to help in His task of teaching the ordinary people, to be the leaven which might work upon this unpromising material and transform it into something approximating to an authentic expression of God's love and God's truth. For he knew that He had been given a unique insight into the meaning of life, into the purposes of God, into the final destiny of man. He knew that He himself was not merely the last and the greatest of the prophets. He came with a mandate from His Father which went beyond anything that had hitherto been known on earth. Dimly, at first, yet with ever increasing clarity He came to see that in and through His life and death the fullness of divine power and divine life would be made available not only to His own people, the Jews, but to the whole of mankind. He was not merely a teacher of a new Way, the revealer of a fuller truth; He was the source of life itself, life ever more abundant.

As the sick and the diseased, the blind and the maimed gathered about Him, His human sympathy and compassion enveloped them with the warmth of His love, and, in so enveloping them, restored them to health and wholeness. Whatever their need, He found that He could always meet it. Then came the day on which He was challenged by the demanding hunger of a vast crowd, numbering thousands of men and women. Their need was compelling; His sympathetic response was more than equal to that need. Under His hands, as He blessed the small supply of bread and fish, the very food was multiplied a thousandfold. Faced with the enthusiasm of the crowd who would have hailed Him there and then as their king, their Messiah, He withdrew from them. What He had done was not the prelude to some dramatic political gesture. He had begun to glimpse a deeper and more permanent reality. As He prayed that evening, He knew what He must do on the morrow.

(iii)

In the synagogue at Capernaum, He began to prepare their minds for the astonishing revelation which had now come to Him and which He must pass on to them. But, first of all,

He must bring them to a realisation that the basic condition for their own fulfilment was that they should accept Him fully, that they should believe in Him as the channel of divine life. As Moses in the desert had saved the people from perishing by giving them the manna, so He himself on the previous day had satisfied their bodily hunger. But these were superficial incidents, meeting a passing need. It was what these events portended and symbolised that really mattered. As the water of Jacob's well had been an image of the well-spring of eternal life, so now the bread, the basic nourishment of man's physical life, must be seen as less real, less significant than the ultimate, the absolute reality which, somehow, He knew himself to be.

He had worked this remarkable miracle. Surely He was entitled to expect, to claim their faith in His power to go far beyond satisfying their passing hunger. Man needed bread, of course. He had recognised this. He had met that need. But man needed so much more. He was suffering from a spiritual hunger, from a deep demand of soul and spirit. The official teachers and leaders of the Jews had shown themselves incapable of meeting this demand. He knew that He could, that He had been commissioned by the Father to do just this. Would they accept this? Would they trust Him sufficiently so that they would lay themselves open to receive the gift of life which was theirs for the asking?

We must presumably see the eucharistic discourse in the sixth chapter of John's gospel as the evangelist's own recollection of what Christ had said rather than a verbatim account. Yet, if it is a reconstruction, it is brilliantly done. We can see Jesus leading His listeners on from an encouragement to believe in Him, to commit themselves to Him as the source of this higher, fuller, more abiding life, on to an acceptance of the idea of their finding in himself the very nourishment they needed. Is it too daring to suggest that when Jesus began to speak in the synagogue that day He did not himself fully realise where the argument would take Him? Even when He ended with the words: 'My flesh is real food, my blood is real drink', could He have known clearly how this statement was to be translated into practical realisation? The very next sentence: 'As I live because of the living Father who has sent me, so he who eats me will live, in his turn, because of me' is hardly a clarification. The relationship between Father and Son is a purely spiritual relationship. How is it possible to argue from that sort of life to the very different procedure whereby a spiritual relationship is established through some sheerly physical communion?

Again, we may ask, is it possible that it was not until that Last Supper with His apostles that the final revelation came to Him? For by now He had come as close as it was possible for Him, even Him, to arrive at a full understanding of all that was involved in this extraordinary partnership between the godhead of the second Person of the Trinity and the humanity of Jesus of Nazareth. More and more, as the years passed, His human consciousness, His human intelligence had been enriched and enlightened by the operation upon it and within it of the eternal Word of God. In speculating about the interrelation of divinity and humanity within the total reality of Christ, it is essential to avoid any suggestion of a purely passive, almost static submissiveness of the elements that went to make up His created nature to the creative power of the divine nature. Just as, even in us, the grace of God respects and, in a mysterious way, is conditioned in its effectiveness by the limitations of our natural being, so must it have been with the Incarnate Word.

He was, at the human, historical level, a product of the Jewish environment in which He had been reared. Naturally, then, His ideas were developments of an already existing body of teaching and practice. Year after year, He had been present at that Passover festival which, as we have seen, was and remains the most significant liturgical activity of the Jewish people and the most powerful force operating to promote their national identity. It would have played a supremely important part in His spiritual development not only as a

Jew but as son of God. Since it was the great expression of God's mighty acts on behalf of His people, it was, for Him, the perfect medium within which to show forth the final consummation of His love, which was the human portrayal of the Creator's love.

Saint John, as we know, in his account of the Last Supper makes no mention of the institution of the Eucharist. What he does emphasise in a way that is peculiar to him is the atmosphere of love in which the proceedings were bathed. He begins the story of those last hours by recalling how Jesus 'loved his own unto the end'. He alone recounts the moving incident of the washing of the disciples' feet; to him alone we are indebted for the superb prayer which is the very testament of Christ's love.

Even if he does not refer directly to the institution of the Eucharist, there is one passage which is not without its relevance. Four times, as we know, during the proceedings a cup of wine is drunk; each time the ritual prayer is said, thanking God, creator of the fruit of the vine. It can hardly be a mere coincidence that one of the most striking passages in the whole of that long prayer is that in which He speaks of himself as the authentic vine, of which His followers are the branches. The life-giving sap, coming from the parent-stock, flows into and through them. One and the same life is the effective force making for that unity between them which reflects and extends the unity between himself and His father. But further, from the fruit of the vine is made the wine which, along with *Afikoman,* is converted into the life-giving flesh and blood of His very self.

(iv)

But does not this imply that throughout Christ is using figurative language? After all, we are not in any literal sense branches of a vine. Why then do we argue that His words about 'body' and 'blood' are to be taken strictly?

Here, of course, we are faced with one of the major problems of interpretation, a problem which has been the occasion for some of the bitterest debates within Western Christendom. This is not the place to consider those debates, though it is well that we should recall an important, indeed an essential principle which applies throughout the whole range of ecumenical discussion. Whatever we may think of the theological opinions and conclusions of those with whom we may disagree, we should always assume that they are no less concerned to defend the truth of Christ's teaching than we are ourselves. We may feel that they are, in fact, betraying that truth. But if we can bring ourselves to give them credit for a genuine Christian concern, this should go far to taking out of our discussions that acrimony which has so often disfigured the relations between theologians of different schools.

How, then, are we to understand Christ's words? There are three main reasons for taking them at their face value. In the first place, when Jesus originally spoke of 'eating his flesh' and 'drinking his blood', the fact that so many of His listeners found the words offensive and literally incredible and that, nevertheless, He did not in any way seek to retain their allegiance by watering down His language is surely proof enough that He really meant what He said. (It is not irrelevant to point out that Jesus was giving a completely different meaning to a familiar expression. To 'drink a man's blood' would mean, to His Jewish listeners, to be revenged on Him, just as we talk about 'thirsting for somebody's blood'. Jesus turned the language of hatred into the language of love.)

In the second place, the apostles themselves must have taken the words literally, since already, within a quarter of a century of the Last Supper, we find Paul writing to the Corinthians in a way which makes sense only if we suppose him to have himself believed that Christ meant His words to be taken literally. Phrases like 'held to account for the Lord's body and blood' and 'not recognising the Lord's body for what it is' (1 Cor. 11: 27 and 29) demand a more than symbolic or metaphorical interpretation.

Finally, of course, the tradition throughout Christendom, both East and West, has been overwhelmingly in favour of thinking of the consecrated elements as no longer mere bread and wine but to be treated as the very body and blood of Christ. It is a simple fact of history that, in the early centuries during which the Church was hammering out her basic trinitarian and christological doctrines (not without considerable and violent disagreement) there seems to have been little or no argument about the eucharist, which, one would have thought, was of more immediate concern to the vast majority of the faithful.

At the same time, it is important not to interpret the words of institution in a crass and ultra-realistic manner. The presence of Christ in the consecrated species is certainly of a different kind from that in which He walked the streets of Nazareth. It is of the nature of our human thinking that all our intellectual activities tend to be accompanied by some degree of pictorial representation, however tenuous. Hence, since the word 'body' has for us an inevitable connotation of bulk, solidity, extension and the like, we almost inevitably transfer these spatial qualities even to Christ's *sacramental* body. For the sophisticated philosopher, reared in the Aristotelian-Scholastic tradition, a term like 'transubstantiation' may be sufficient to guard against any suggestion of solidity or crass corporeality. For the man in the street, to whom 'substance' is something that can be weighed and measured, the term can be misleading.

As so often happens with the profoundest truths, we can be precise more by denial than by affirmation. Thus, we must begin by making it clear that any suggestion of cannibalism, a literal eating of Christ's flesh in the way in which we eat the flesh of animals, is certainly ruled out. Indeed whatever we may do to the consecrated species in no way affects Christ himself. The effect is in us. The effect is in us, precisely because we are in direct and immediate communication with the total reality that Christ is. We are present to Him; He is present to us. Therefore, since He is body no less than spirit, human no less than divine, He must be present in a bodily and human way, in order that His spiritual, divine power may be communicated to us through the medium of His sacramental presence.

But the very debate about the *manner* of Christ's bodily presence does very little service to the essential purpose of that presence, which is the communication of that eternal life which goes far beyond the physical life of a human body. Serious damage to the purity of eucharistic doctrine has been done by stories, popular in the middle ages, about bleeding hosts and visions of small children seen in the consecrated wafer. Christ's presence is not that sort of reality. All we can say is that, genuine and actual as is the presence of Christ in the consecrated elements, it is a unique sort of presence. Such a term as 'transubstantiation' does not mean, for example, that the molecular structure of the bread undergoes any sort of change. We are in a world of discourse where scientific terminology is of no avail. Nor does philosophy help either. If the poet is right when he says

> Philosophy can clip an angel's wings . . .
> Unweave a rainbow

it can almost take the mysteriousness out of mystery. Fortunately we are saved not by philosophy but by faith.

CHAPTER III

FROM PASSOVER TO PASSION

'If then these sacrifices cleanse the copies of heavenly things, those heavenly things themselves require better sacrifices to cleanse them. For Christ has entered not that sanctuary made by men's hands, which is only a symbol of the reality, but heaven itself, to appear now before God on our behalf.' Hebrews 9: 23–5.

'Offering was the decisive part of sacrifice: sin-offerings called for the slaying of the victim, but while the slaying might be done by others (the Temple servants, for instance), only the priest could make the offering. So that Isaiah [53: 10] is speaking of a sacrifice in which Priest and Victim were one person. In our thinking we tend to concentrate on Christ as victim, but His torturing and slaying was the work of His enemies. Their slaying Him would have made Him a martyr, but not a sacrificial victim. Only His own offering did that.' F. J. Sheed, *What Difference does Jesus Make?* pp. 175–6.

(i)

We human beings are prisoners of both space and time. Even though our thought can range up and down the centuries or project itself to the limits of the uttermost galaxy, we can never quite shake off the feeling that all reality must be conditioned, as we are conditioned, stretching however far into the past and the future, from one edge of the universe to another. So we need ever to remind ourselves that these are diminishments of existence. The higher we rise in the scale of being, the more do we realise that greater liberty and more

35

powerful intelligence are marked by an increasing independence of these limitations. Extrapolating from this view, we can argue that the perfect being that God is must be totally unaffected by the restrictions of space and time.

It is in the light of such considerations that we can continue our investigation into the depths of the eucharistic mystery. For that mystery is incomprehensible to us precisely because, whilst it is present to us in our space-time experience, in itself it transcends all such restrictions. Already in the Upper Room, whilst, in His human nature, Christ was still subjected to the limitations of our mortality, His sacramental presence was not so subjected. We do not have to suppose that He was doubled or multiplied twelve times as He broke and distributed the *Afikoman* that had now—by His power—been fulfilled by being transformed from anticipation to actuality.

Equally, in his sacramental actuality, he could speak of His body 'given up' for us, His blood 'shed' for us, although the surrender and the blood-shedding had not yet, as a matter of history, taken place. It is here that we come to the other, deeper, more important aspect of the meaning of the eucharist, its relation to the one sacrifice of our redemption. Even more than the arguments about the 'how' of Christ's presence in the consecrated species, the debate about the sacrificial significance of the eucharistic liturgy has divided church from church and Christian from Christian. Is it possible, after centuries of controversy, when every aspect of the problem would seem to have been exhausted, to take another look at this topic and find some mutual understanding?

We talk readily enough about the atoning, redemptive value of the crucifixion of Jesus. Our sins, we are told, are washed away in the blood of the Lamb. Through His death we are reconciled to God. All Christians are at one in accepting the idea that the sufferings and death of Christ are the essential factor in that process whereby man, alienated from God by sin, has found his way back to the divine favour. Is it possible to get behind the traditional language and come to a fresh appraisal of the underlying truth?

Let us begin by looking at the situation from which man needed to be redeemed. In other words, let us try to see what we mean by sin. This would seem a naïve and unnecessary suggestion. After all we have more than enough experience of sin in our lives. Do we really need to ask what it is?

Well, do I possibly think of sin primarily, if not exclusively, in terms of something that happens to me, something that I 'fall into', something that I do—or refuse to do? Superficially, this is all true enough as a description of what one may call the outward appearance of sin. But the sinful conduct is sinful precisely because, and only because, it is a manifestation of an attitude of mind. Sin is not so much something that I do as something that I have become. Two more or less indistinguishable actions can be performed by different individuals (or by the same individual at different times) one of which may be sinful and the other not. A surgeon can stick a knife into a man and be doing a laudable action. Not so the murderer, who might, for example, dress up as a surgeon and use a surgeon's scalpel to achieve his murderous purpose. As so often happens, we have to get behind the appearance to penetrate to the reality.

(ii)

What, in the end, makes sin sinful is that the act (or omission) is inspired, more or less deliberately, by an attitude of disobedience, of refusal to do what I know to be right. When Milton spoke of 'Man's first disobedience' he was referring to the refusal of Adam and Eve to accept God's restriction on their liberty. Whatever we may think of the historical value of the story as told in the third chapter of Genesis, we cannot fail to see its profound moral and spiritual significance. 'You shall be as gods' is the temptation to which man has been subjected from the beginning of time, the temptation to be independent, to be a law to himself, to be subject to no one. But since man is, by his very created nature, subject to the divine command which is, at the same time, the law of his own being, his very disobedience to that command means inevitably that he is doing harm to his own nature.

When preachers and others talk about God 'punishing sin', or being made 'angry' by man's sin, they are in fact using metaphorical language. The simple truth is that what is called the 'punishment' of sin is, so to say, built into the system. If a heavy smoker contracts lung cancer, I can say, if I like, that he is 'being punished' for smoking too heavily. If a motorist takes a bend too fast, leaves the road and smashes himself against a tree, again I can say he is 'being punished' for reckless driving. (Though, if he kills someone else in the process, are we right in supposing that the second party is also being punished for the driver's recklessness?) The consequences of our actions are what they are. The consequences of sinful actions may, in the short run, seem to bring some immediate satisfaction, some profit, some benefit to the individual. But the history of the world should bear eloquent testimony to the fact that human selfishness and greed and cruelty have brought untold misery into the human lot. In other words what we call the punishment of sin is not something inflicted on man from outside by a capricious deity. It is a direct consequence of man's disregard of the health warning on the packet, an outcome as predictable as the car smash suffered by the foolish driver.

So, too, when we talk about 'God's anger'. The unchanging, ceaseless love of God for His creatures is not in any degree diminished by their unworthiness. What does happen when man sins is that he erects, on his side, a barrier cutting off the *effects* of that love. If mankind lived up to its responsibilities, if all men treated their fellow-men with that sympathy and compassion which they ought to display, the effects of God's love for His children would be universally effective. But, as it is, all men, to a greater or less extent, have raised those

barriers which shut out the divine benevolence. In that sense
it is as though God were angry. The world, in effect, cannot
be influenced by the love of God so long as man resists,
disobeys.

If then it is the case that in essence sin is an attitude of
disobedience, it can be repaired only by obedience. And here
we approach the heart of the redemptive work of Christ. But
again we need to examine our language with care. When
St. Paul says of Christ that 'he became obedient unto death,
even death on a cross' (Phil. 2 : 8), he must not be taken to
mean that the Father ordered the Son to die by crucifixion
and that the Son obeyed the order. The situation was not quite
so simple, nor so shocking.

(iii)

In so far as it is possible for us to understand the way in
which our redemption was achieved, the truth seems to be
something like this. In the first place, it seems more in keep-
ing with what we know of God's dealings with His creature,
man, to accept the teaching of Scotus that the Incarnation,
far from being a sort of afterthought on God's part, a healing
action required by the need to rescue man from the predica-
ment into which he had got himself, was all along part of
the crowning gift of God's creative love. Since we must
explain the whole creative process as an expression 'beyond'
the Godhead of that inexhaustible self-giving, that love which
is the essence of the divine nature, it seems natural to assume
that that love would go to the limit in its self-giving. That
limit is best seen in the literal self-giving whereby the
creator entered into the created realm, to share man's
experience and man's nature. The eternal Word of God, fully
divine, became fully human. To be fully human meant to be
born of woman, at a certain moment in time, in a given
situation—and to accept the consequences of such a com-
mittal. What we call Christ's obedience must be seen as His
submission to what we may call the law of the Incarnation.

Becoming man, He could not refuse to accept the conditions of mortality without disobedience to that law.

Sin, as we have seen, is essentially disobedience, the refusal of service, the refusal to respond to the demands of human life in a fully human way. Its counterpart, redemption from sin, is the acceptance of those demands. But the demands are not pre-ordained by God. They are imposed on us, as they were imposed on Jesus, by the circumstances of life, and in particular by the conduct of our fellow-men. We saw in a previous chapter what was involved for Jesus in the particular situation in which His life was lived. It is now appropriate to look at certain aspects of that situation in a little more detail.

Take for example the incident of the first of the three 'temptations', the suggestion that Jesus should turn stones into bread. In what sense must we think of this as a temptation? Clearly, in itself the performance of such a simple miracle could hardly be wrong. After all, at a later stage, He was to work a far more remarkable miracle in multiplying the loaves. The difference lies in the fact that in this instance He was being invited to work a miracle on His own behalf. To have listened to the suggestion would have been to let himself off the conditions of normal human existence. Ordinary human beings are not in a position to alleviate their distress by having recourse to superhuman, miraculous powers. So with Jesus. By submitting to the normal conditions of human living He demonstrated the reality of His obedience to what we have called the law of the Incarnation. Only so could He assure us of the completeness of His identification of himself with us. That is why, throughout His life, we see Him subjected to what is most characteristic of human experience—hard work, insecurity, sorrow, pain and finally death. (There were, of course, other characteristic features—human love, joy, delight in the beauties of creation and so on. Our picture of Jesus must be a balanced one if it is to be truly a portrayal of one who was 'like us in all things but for sin'.)

Remembering the complex religious and political situation of Palestine in the days of Christ, we can see how the manner of His death was all but inevitable. Any one of three factors could have delivered Him from such a terrible end. Either He himself might have lost heart and ceased to 'bear witness to the truth', which was His duty as He saw it. But such an act of weakness would have been a denial of His authentic manhood. Or, the Father might have sent 'twelve legions of angels' to rescue Him. But that would have been to frustrate the whole purpose of the Incarnation. Or, thirdly, the Jewish leaders might have come to accept Him—just as Pilate might have stood up to the crowd and said: 'No, this man is innocent; I will not allow Him to be put to death.' But, unless these human agents had so freely chosen, crucifixion had to be.

The obedience of Christ, then, is not to some explicit demand of the Father. It is to be seen as His response to the detailed demands imposed on Him by His contemporaries. Clearly, to suppose that the Father had directly willed the death of His Son is to suppose that the Father also willed the sin of those who perpetrated that crime.

(iv)

But, it will be asked, what are we to make of Christ's prayer in the Garden: 'Father, if it be possible, let this chalice pass from me; only, not my will but yours must be done'. Surely, it would seem, the words imply that it was foreordained that He should drink that chalice to the dregs. But nothing is foreordained in the sense that human beings are not left free to make their own decisions. It was, theoretically, still possible for Caiaphas to have a change of heart; it was still possible for Pilate to find the necessary courage. Only, unless something like this happened, what would be, would be. Similar considerations apply to the prophecies that foretold the sufferings of Christ. Again, we need not suppose that men's freedom is taken away from them because their conduct has been foretold. On the contrary, it was because they were going, freely, to choose to act in this way that the prophecies had in fact been made.

If then we ask why it was necessary for Christ to suffer in this terrible way, the answer is, in the words of the Creed, 'for us men', *propter nos homines.* As we have seen, so long as the conditions were what they were, these things would come to pass. A dramatic intervention by the Father, a refusal on the part of the Son would have left us dissatisfied. For our sakes, to convince us, He had to go through with it.

To convince *us.* There are times, as we contemplate the life and death of Jesus, when we are inclined to think, perhaps we have been encouraged to think, that He was proving something to His Father. If we think this, we totally fail to understand the situation. Whilst it is true that we human beings need to have things demonstrated to us, need to see people behave in certain ways before we are able to appreciate their worth, the reverse is true of God. God knows, sees, the quality of a human being altogether apart from the way in which that human being behaves. We can hardly suppose that the Father was waiting for the Son to do certain things, to accept suffering, to die in agony before He could be 'satisfied'. Indeed, Thomas Aquinas goes so far as to say that one single act of Christ's human will would have sufficed to redeem the entire world. Alas, the Father might have been satisfied; not we. To prove *to us* the completeness of His humanity, the total lack of any kind of reservation in His commitment to our human condition, He drained the chalice of suffering and death to the dregs.

Yet, if there is any meaning at all in the doctrine of the Redemption or the Atonement, the idea that, through Christ's death, mankind is restored to God's favour, that sacrificial death must have been of significance to the Father also. What can that significance be like?

Here, of course, we are at the heart of the mystery, inevitably baffled by our human attempt to enter into the mind of God. Nevertheless the attempt must be made, if such terms as redemption, atonement, reconciliation and the like are to be more than purely nebulous concepts. We have already seen that the need for redemption arises from the fact of man's opposition to God through the disobedience that sin essentially is. Redemption, reconciliation, must be the antithesis of this. Man can be put right with God only if his hostility is turned into acceptance, his disobedience into obedience. This is why, throughout His life, Christ insisted that He had come to do His Father's will, that His very food was that same will (John 4: 34; Matt. 4: 4). What that meant in practice, as we have also seen, was the faithful submission to the demands of life, in a human context, as these demands successively disclosed themselves.

(v)

One important aspect of this whole situation is the fact that the redemption was something that was achieved from within mankind. That is to say, we must not think of God as waving a sort of merciful wand and forgiving man his sins. It was, and is, necessary to an understanding of God's dealing with us that we should see how He so respects our freedom of choice that, whilst recognising our responsibility for our sinful deeds, He has also made it possible for us to work out our own salvation. True as it is that, without the divine initiative, this would not have been possible, we must nevertheless appreciate the truth that that same initiative was such as to put it into man's own power, to make man himself capable of responding in such a way as to obey rather than disobey, to accept rather than reject, to choose the way of life rather than the way of death.

When St. Paul says: 'It is all God's work. . . . God in Christ was reconciling the world to himself' (2 Cor. 5: 18–19), we must not interpret the words in a sense which will tend to obscure the reality of the contribution made by the humanity of the Incarnate Word. One of the earliest heresies rejected by the Church was the Docetic teaching that Christ only appeared to possess a human nature, a sort of actor's mask which He wore as He went through the motions of playing the part of a human being. So, at a later stage, did she reject the Monophysite heresy which held that it was only the divine nature that mattered, that the very presence of the godhead effectively overwhelmed the humanity, which could make no serious contribution to the work of Christ. The orthodox view which has prevailed is that, whilst the value of Christ's work is infinitely enhanced by the fact that the humanity is intimately linked with the divinity, nevertheless it is precisely the work of Jesus of Nazareth, the son of Mary, which is the necessary element in the work of our redemption.

(vi)

We must now turn to consider one aspect of the religious and spiritual development of Jesus a little more precisely. Within the general context of those scriptural ideas which, as we have already seen, held for Him a personal and immediate meaning such as to shape His whole attitude to life, we may single out for special consideration the texts relating to the redemptive work which He knew himself called upon to perform. Throughout Jewish history, indeed in the Jewish understanding of man's pre-Jewish religious experience, the notion of sacrifice had always played a central role in life. The first reference to it is, of course, in the story of the sons of Adam, Cain and Abel, bringing their respective produce, fruits and lambs, as an offering to God. So, too, after the Flood Noah offered animals and birds, whose 'appeasing fragrance' was acceptable to God.

In the early chapters of Leviticus, elaborate instructions are laid down for various forms of sacrifice. The basic notion underlying them all is that they are various ways of expressing symbolically man's recognition of God's dominion over

44

all things, especially over life itself. Since 'the life of the flesh is in the blood' (Lev. 17: 11), the blood of any animal that was sacrificed had to be poured round the altar, as a sign of its special sacredness. On the Day of Atonement the High Priest took blood into the Holy of Holies to sprinkle it on the Ark of the Covenant. (In this connection, we may notice the passage in Exodus (24: 1–11), telling the story of the ratification of the Covenant. Apparently combining two traditions, it describes how Moses took the blood of the sacrifice, poured half of it over the altar and the other half in the direction of the people; but it also tells of a meal which he and the elders of the people ate in the presence of God.)

If we ask why the destruction of produce could be regarded as symbolic of God's dominion, the answer runs something like this. That which belongs to another does not belong to me. It is, strictly speaking, beyond my control. Thus, by destroying that which is precious, I symbolise this truth by literally putting it beyond my control. It never has been 'mine', absolutely. It can no longer be mine in any sense. Chesterton has expressed this idea in characteristic fashion in his poem about the gifts of the Wise Men:

> 'We say he has no more to gain, but we have less to lose,
> Less gold shall go astray, we say, less gold if thus we choose . . .
> And if our hands are glad, O God, to cast them down like flowers,
> 'Tis not that they enrich thy hands, but they are saved from ours.'

But the notion of reparation, of repentance, of being rid of sin is another significant element in the theory and practice of sacrifice. Since God is the supreme lord of creation, any misuse of creatures is an encroachment on His sovereignty. It follows that, if I am to make things right, to restore the situation, I must re-affirm my recognition of God's dominion.

This is done by further sacrificial offerings. Also in the Jewish tradition, there survived the notion of the scapegoat, literally bearing away the sins of the people.

> 'Aaron must lay his hands on its head and confess all the faults of the sons of Israel, all their transgressions and their sins, and lay them to its charge. Having thus laid them on the goat's head, he shall send it out into the desert . . . and the goat will bear away all their faults with it into a desert place' (Lev. 16: 21–2).

(vii)

In course of time, as tends to happen in all religious traditions, the external ceremony came to be thought of as somehow effective in its own right. One of the constant themes of the prophets was the need for a change of heart to make the sacrifices meaningful.

> 'What are your endless sacrifices to me? says Yahweh.
> I am sick of holocausts of rams
> and the fat of calves. . . .
> Take your wrong-doing out of my sight.
> Cease to do evil.
> Learn to do good' (Is. 1: 10–17).
> 'What I want is love not sacrifice,
> knowledge of God, not holocausts' (Hos. 6: 6).

In the rabbinic tradition, the same view was expressed in the words: 'Death and the Day of Atonement are effective if there is repentance'.

Perhaps it is in Psalm 51, traditionally ascribed to David, that we find the most moving expression of this truth.

> 'Sacrifice gives you no pleasure,
> were I to offer holocaust
> you would not have it.
> My sacrifice is this broken spirit,
> you will not scorn this crushed and broken heart.'

46

In another psalm, the same idea is expressed:

> 'You asked no holocaust or sacrifice for sin;
> Then I said: Here I am, I am coming.
> In the scroll of the book, am I not commanded
> to obey your will' (Ps. 40: 6–7).

Again we must picture Jesus, seeing himself as the son of David, applying to himself these and similar passages. During His long years at Nazareth, as He meditated on such texts, He came to see more and more clearly the nature of His calling. First of all, like the prophets of old, He must recall His people to a deeper understanding of their religious tradition. Bearing witness to the truth, He must make man realise the nature of His Father and theirs, make them see that the whole purpose of the Law, the liturgy, their destiny as the Chosen People was that they, above all, must practise an authentic worship, in spirit and in truth.

So He came to see how He would bring together in himself the variegated strands of that religious teaching, bring them together and, in so blending them, give a new impetus, a new dimension to man's quest for God. The ritual of circumcision, by which Israel had been bound to God in a Covenant by which God had bound himself to Israel, was no mere symbol. It had been practised on Him, in whom mankind and not just the Jewish people had become intimately united with the God of Abraham. The enactments of the Torah, to which He submitted in all its detail, must yet be shown, not as a negative, restricting infringement of man's freedom but as the very condition of the full exercise of that freedom, not as a burden under which man made his painful way but as an inspiring and joyous surrender to the loving appeal of God. Supremely, in him would be finally realised everything that the great Temple ritual stood for. One of His memories of that first visit to Jerusalem could well have been the sight of the sacrificial lambs being driven through the Sheep Gate to be slaughtered in the Temple area. When

John the Baptist hailed Him as the Lamb of God, He had already begun to realise how His life would end.

When therefore at that last meal with His chosen company, the new Assembly of God, He took the bread and the wine, He was not just leaving them a visible, tangible memorial of His sojourning among men. He was associating them with himself in the final sacrifice which was to be his final achievement. 'In the world you will have hardship; but, be of good heart: I am the conqueror of the world' (John 16: 33). The Messiah, the Lord's anointed, a greater than Solomon, king not only of the Jewish nation but of all mankind, would be enthroned the next day, lifted up on the Cross. In the Hallel which they were shortly to sing together occur the words:

> 'The Lord is with me, I will not fear:
>> what can man do unto me?
> I shall not die but live:
>> and declare the works of the Lord. . . .
> The stone which the builders rejected
>> has become the keystone' (Ps. 118: 17, 22).

So, too, those great passages from Isaiah would be running through His mind, passages foretelling the sufferings of the Servant (the servant who had just been washing the feet of His brethren), but containing that great assurance:

> 'See, my servant will prosper,
>> He shall be lifted up, exalted, rise to great heights'
>>> (Is. 52: 13).

It was not that His sufferings were not real, not something to be dreaded. In the garden and on the cross, even His superb courage seemed, for a space, to be on the verge of breaking. So it must be if He was to be still the fully human victim of man's cruelty, jealousy, selfishness, ambition, blindness, duplicity and greed. Not for Him the Stoic contempt of feeling. It is through our feelings that we can best enter into another's experience. So was it with Him. 'Ours

were the sufferings he bore, ours the sorrows he carried'
(Is. 53 : 4). Supported by His faith in the loving providence
of God, which even He could not always, humanwise, understand, He knew that in and through this final trial of His
human spirit, humanity itself would emerge into a brighter
light, a richer inheritance.

D

CHAPTER IV

FROM PASSION TO PENTECOST

'We saw his glory, the glory that is his as the Father's only Son.' John 1 : 14.

'The Resurrection narratives are not a picture of survival after death; they record how a totally new mode of being had appeared in the universe. Something new had appeared in the universe: as new as the first coming of organic life. This Man, after death, does not get divided into "ghost" and "corpse". A new mode of being has arisen.' C. S. Lewis, *Undeceptions,* p. 126.

(i)

Tetelestai. The Greek form of our Lord's last word from the Cross can be rendered into English only in a cumbersome way. 'The purpose of my life has been achieved' perhaps comes nearest to its meaning. He had finished the work His Father had given Him to do. He had met all the demands that life had made on Him. He had been fully obedient to the will of God in that, in every situation that had confronted Him, He had behaved in a way that was totally human, not in the sense that He had displayed any sort of human weakness or folly, but in the sense that He had always risen to the height of the challenge. In Him therefore human nature was revealed in its essential integrity; in Him, in theological language, human nature was redeemed.

Now, what is absolutely central to an understanding of the whole economy of the redemption is the recognition of the fact that it was not what Christ did or suffered which, in itself, restored the situation. It was what He was. When we thought about sin, we came to see that sin is not, in itself, something that we do; it is something that we become. It is the disobedience, the underlying attitude of will, which gives sin its malice. So was it with the redemptive work of our Lord. We know that two other men were crucified along with Him, experiencing approximately the same suffering, feeling the same pain, meeting death by His side. What distinguished His death from theirs and gave it its sacrificial meaning and value was the fact that, as He himself said, no one took His life from Him: He 'laid it down' of His own free will.

In other words, to dwell too much on the physical aspect of the Passion, to speak of the shedding of the precious blood of Christ as, exclusively or even primarily, the means of our redemption is to make the sort of mistake which the Jews of old made when they came to think of their sacrifices as important-in-themselves, without reference to the spirit in which they were made. Unfortunately we human beings are only too prone to fall into this sort of materialism, to think of the action, the object, the thing, the place as sacred in and of themselves. Our Lord, we remember, contrasted worship 'in spirit and in truth' with worship in the Temple whether at Jerusalem or on Mount Gerazim. Things and places can be helps, means; they betray their purpose when they are idolised.

There is another reason why we must not dwell over-much on the events of the Passion, on Calvary, on the Cross as though all this was, is, all that mattered. It is indeed true that, as the risen Lord himself said: 'Christ had to suffer— and thereby enter into his glory' (Luke 24: 26). But we separate the glory from the suffering if we remain contemplating the Cross without looking through it to the Life beyond it, to the completion, the fulfilment achieved by it. As St. Paul says in a well known yet ever to be meditated passage:

'His state was divine;
yet he did not cling to his equality with God,

51

but emptied himself to assume the condition of a slave,
and became as men are;
being what all men are
he was humbler yet
even to accepting death, death on a cross.
But God raised him high and gave him the name which
is above all other names
so that all beings,
in the heavens, on earth and under the earth,
should bend the knee at the name of Jesus,
and that every tongue should acclaim
Jesus Christ as Lord
to the glory of God the Father' (Phil. 2 : 6–11).

In the incident of the Transfiguration, when Peter and his two companions saw His glory, we have a glimpse of a transient experience, an anticipatory indication of that eternal glory, into which Christ himself would finally enter, and to which all men are called. The second of the two letters attributed to Peter makes this event the occasion for an inspiring comment:

'By his divine power he, our saviour Jesus Christ, has given us all the things we need for life and for true religion, bringing us to know God himself, who has called us by his own glorious power. . . . We had seen him with our own eyes in majesty, when God the Father honoured and glorified him, when the Sublime Glory itself spoke to him and said: This is my dear Son; he enjoys my favour' (Pet. 1: 3, 16–17).

Behind both these passages may well lie an idea familiar to the Rabbis. In a Jewish writing entitled the *Apocalypse of Moses*, Eve reproaches Adam, after he had (at her suggestion) eaten of the forbidden fruit: 'I know that I am stripped of the righteousness with which I had been clothed, and I wept and I said to him (Adam): "Why have you done this to me depriving me of the glory that clothed me?" '. Commenting on the passage a rabbinic commentary explained: 'Through Adam's sin, the *shekinah* (God's glory and presence) withdrew to the first heaven; man's actual sins drove it still further away'. In other words, man's disobedience had dimmed the brightness of God's glorious presence in the world and in man himself. The obedience of Christ restored that brightness, though the persisting effects of sin would still obscure it for man's vision, until, at the end of time, Christ should return 'on the clouds of glory' (Matt. 26: 64), a phrase which recalls the vision of Daniel:

> 'I saw coming on the clouds of heaven
> one like a son of man . . .
> On him was conferred sovereignty,
> glory and kingship,
> and men of all peoples, nations and languages became
> his servants.
> His sovereignty is an eternal sovereignty
> which shall never pass away,
> nor will his empire ever be destroyed' (Dan. 7: 13–14).

(ii)

Yet the first stage in the glorification of Christ, His Resurrection, is almost surprising in its apparent ordinariness. Not only did He declare himself 'in the breaking of bread', show His doubtful disciples the wounds still to be seen on His flesh, invite Thomas to handle Him; in John's description of His appearance on the lake-side, the atmosphere is almost one of a family picnic, as though the risen Lord would remind His followers that the glory that awaited them, the glory which He won for them, was not yet. For them, there remained the task of carrying His message to the ends of the earth, living on in faith, in the certainty of ultimate triumph even if, for them, as for Him, the way to glory was the path of duty, of obedience, of witness to the truth by the testimony of blood.

Certainly, they still needed much enlightenment. Even after the events of the Passion and Resurrection, after the forty days during which He had continued to appear to them and give them further instruction about the kingdom, they could still think in terms of political power. 'Lord, has the time come?' We can hear the eagerness in their voices. 'Are you going to restore the kingdom to Israel?' (Acts 1 : 6). He might well have repeated what He had said to them after the Supper:

'I still have many things to say to you,
but they would be too much for you now.
But when the Spirit of truth comes
he will lead you to the complete truth'

(John 16: 12–13)

So He was taken away from them, leaving them feeling bereft. Yet, as He had already warned them, it was for their own good that He was going.

'Unless I go,
the Advocate will not come to you' (John 16: 7).

So long as He was there, they would have gone on thinking in terms of the sort of Messianism which meant some sort of earthly glory. He had shown His power over death. No earthly power, not even the power of Rome, could withstand such authority. Left to themselves, though 'in the power of the Spirit', they would realise the true nature of the kingdom they were to preach.

(iii)

The Fifty Days which began with the sacrificial death of Jesus on Calvary ended with the tempestuous, fiery coming of the Spirit. The Church was born. Its marks were a common faith in the teaching of the apostles, that 'witness' which Jesus had enjoined on them; a unity in that mutual love which had been His supreme commandment; the eucharistic meal; a life of prayer (Acts 2 : 42). All four were different aspects of a basic reality, the ongoing life of Jesus. For that life was the outcome of faith in Him; the mutual love was a manifestation of His love in them; the eucharist was the outward, visible sign of His vitalising power; prayer was the evidence of faith : 'to invoke the name of Christ' is the sign of the Christian.

Singling out for our present study the primitive practice of meeting together in their houses to 'break bread', we may find it helpful if we try to enter into the minds of those first believers and picture their thoughts and feelings at these eucharistic services. It is not our purpose to institute a liturgical enquiry; the material is not available. Nor indeed can we construct a 'theology of the eucharist' in any but the most general terms. But certain facts which are perhaps not always borne in mind may bring us to a better appreciation of what this ceremony must have meant at this early stage in the Church's life.

Whatever date we may assign to the final editing of the book of the Acts, it is surely difficult to read these early chapters without getting a sense of immediacy, of the freshness of dawn. It reflects the mentality of a community that was conscious of living in two worlds, the old world of the Temple worship (Acts 2 : 44; 3 : 1; 5 : 12, 20, 21, 42) and the new world of the glorified Son of Man, present no longer exclusively in the *shekinah* of Yahweh, but here in their midst, wherever two or three were gathered in His name, supremely in the breaking of bread.

We begin then by recalling that those first celebrations of the eucharist were conducted by men who had seen and heard Jesus take the *Afikoman* and pronounce over it those words which declared that it had now found its fulfilment in Him. Neither the apostles themselves nor their followers asked metaphysical questions. It was enough for them that Jesus, who had 'the message of eternal life', had said 'Do this in remembrance of me'. But what were they consciously remembering? Only a matter of weeks ago, this same Jerusalem was ringing with the story of the condemnation, the sufferings, the death of Jesus. The last time they had celebrated the Passover, that memorial of the great deliverance from Egypt, was also the first time Jesus had brought home to them the reality of their liberation, not from slavery and oppression, but from the burden of their sins.

But they remembered, too, the more astonishing events that had ensued. Some of them had actually seen the Risen Lord, not just the Twelve, but those five hundred to whom Paul was to refer in his letter to the Corinthians, twenty-five years hence. All this was vividly present to them, so vivid that it was scarcely a memory. It was all but a direct experience Yet it was not the facts that mattered, so much as what the facts stood for. For they meant that, even if His earthly life had come to an end, He still lived on in himself and in them. The past was important only as an assurance, a guarantee of a present reality, a foreshadowing of what was to be. If He had withdrawn from them for a while, He would be coming back to them, to take them with Him into the glory of His Father and His own. Past, present and future merged for them into one abiding truth. Jesus is alive: we too live by His life.

At the same time, we must not lose sight of the fact that, at this stage of the Church's history, the Christian community was composed almost exclusively of men and women who had been reared, like Jesus himself, in the Jewish tradition. Inevitably, they would see themselves as still within the great Jewish family, they would interpret the teaching and work of Jesus from a strictly Jewish standpoint. The new Covenant could not abrogate the old: God ever remained faithful to His promises. Yet, just as Moses and the prophets had developed and deepened the initial covenant, so had Jesus enriched and fulfilled it in a way which was a true renewal. The Temple still stood and with it all the requirements of the ritual law had to be complied with. Yet, side by side with the continuing daily sacrifices within the splendour of Herod's magnificent construction, they knew that these sacrifices were no more than anticipations, prefigurings of the supreme sacrifice in which the Lamb of God had offered His life that all men might live. They had been prepared for this final revelation by the teaching and the practice of their priests and doctors. Saddened as they were to think that their leaders had failed to accept Jesus as the Messiah, the saviour of Israel, they still felt a sense of loyalty to a tradition which had meant so much to them. In an important sense, it was their very Jewishness which provided the framework within which the developing Christian consciousness might fashion a new and deeper unity, a unity that was all the more significant because it no longer depended on racial or social factors.

CHAPTER V

FRAGMENTATION

'Has Christ been divided up?' 1 Corinthians 1 : 13.

'As an historian I am convinced that the main sources of Christian division and the chief obstacle to Christian unity have been and are cultural rather than theological. Consequently, I believe that it is only by combining the study of the history of Christian culture with the study of theology that we can understand the nature and extent of the problem with which we have to deal.' Christopher Dawson, *The Dividing of Christendom*, p. 17.

(i)

The first time we meet with disagreement among Christians in connection with the eucharist is, perhaps surprisingly, not a linguistic or theological one. Writing to the Corinthians, Paul has occasion to upbraid them for the way in which they behave at gatherings which are meant to be like those of the very first Christian converts who 'met in their houses for the breaking of bread' (Acts 2: 46). Unfortunately, unlike them, who 'shared their food gladly and generously', the Corinthian assemblies had become a cause of division and discrimination, not because the members disagreed about the interpretation of Christ's word, but because they were selfish, uncharitable, ostentatious and intemperate. (A similar situation, indicated in Jude v. 12, reminds us that the first generation of Christians were not exempt from the frailties of human nature.) The interesting point is that Paul appeals to the reality of Christ's bodily presence as an argument that should bring about an improvement in their behaviour. 'Anyone who eats the bread or drinks the cup of the Lord unworthily will be guilty of desecrating the body and blood of the Lord' (1 Cor. 11 : 27). Although he does remind his readers of the story of the institution, he does not argue about the nature of Christ's presence or try to explain how it is possible. The facts argue for themselves.

Indeed it was some considerable time before the effort to systematise a theology of the eucharist was made. As Professor Lampe puts it:

> 'The chief reason for the paucity of theological exposi-
> tions of the eucharist in the early period, and the
> reasons why the Christian writers' occasional allusions
> to it are difficult to analyse systematically, is that the
> Eucharist stands at the heart of the early Church's faith
> and life; it embodies and proclaims in a single rite the
> entire richness of the gospel; and for this very reason
> it does not lend itself to precise definition or to clear-
> cut theories about presence, sacrifice, consecration, and
> the relation of the sacramental act and of the visible
> elements to the reality which they signify.'

It is not our purpose to trace out the development of a eucharistic theology or to assess the value (or the orthodoxy) of various statements. Important as theological enquiry is, it suffers from all man's attempts to reduce reality to a set of formulae. Browning's words about 'fancies that broke through language and escaped' must ever remind us that language is a useful tool; it is not the master of our thinking. Discussion is useful if it liberates the truth, helps us to a deeper understanding of a reality which will never be finally stated in a definitive formula. The theological babel which has so deafened the Church down the centuries is a con-sequence of the attitude of mind which inspired the builders of the original ziggurat:

'They said to one another, "Come, let us make bricks and bake them hard"; they used bricks for stone, for mortar they used bitumen. "Come", they said, "let us build ourselves a city with a tower that reaches to heaven, and make a name for ourselves . . . " ' (Gen. 11: 1–3).

Theology can never reach up to heaven nor can the truth of God be compressed into hard bricks—bricks which are so often used to hurl at rival scholars.

(ii)

The following considerations, then, are advanced in the hope that they may help Christians, whose common devotion to Christ has been fragmented by conflicting theories, definitions, formulations to approach one another in a united effort to worship together once more in spirit and in truth. They will not, they do not seek to provide a statement of a commonly accepted doctrine. Perhaps they will at least take some of the bitterness out of a controversy whose very existence belies the sacred truth which allegedly gave rise to it. Like those Corinthians our divisions are not really intellectual. They are due to moral factors which, if less crude than the vices which disrupted the *agape* at Corinth, are not less harmful to that Christian love which we all profess.

No Christian who accepts any sort of eucharistic doctrine and practice believes in the Real Absence. (It is fitting that Dr. John Huxtable who originally made this remark to the author should receive the credit for it.) In other words, we all believe that, in some sense, Christ is actively present in the sacred elements which are at the centre of our worship. Presumably, those who have disagreed and fought about the way in which Christ can be present, is present, must be present, all believe that they are thus safeguarding the essential truth about which they are all equally concerned. Even when they flatly contradict one another, what they are in fact contradicting is some statement which, as they suppose, is incompatible with Christ's own teaching—to which by their profession they are committed. What they are forgetting is that the essential mystery eludes and must always elude definition. As Teilhard de Chardin said, though not explicitly in this context: 'Doctrinal formulations falsify by what they omit'. In safeguarding one aspect of the truth, perhaps the aspect which I believe to be fundamental, I may well suggest to those brought up in another tradition a misrepresentation, a falsification, by omission.

Take, for example, the term 'transubstantiation' which Roman Catholic theology has officially endorsed as the best way of summarising what takes place in the eucharistic act. What was bread is now the Body of Christ. What was the substance we call bread is now the substance we call flesh. Therefore the process is best described as a process of change of substance, 'transubstantiation'. We have already seen that, helpful as this term may have been for the philosopher who thought of substance as something which is different from the qualities of solidity, extension, resistance and the like, it is necessarily misleading to those who think of substance precisely as something in itself solid, extended, resistant and so forth. The fact that, in the Creed, they readily apply the term to God, Father and Son, 'sharing one substance', does not help, although substance in this case clearly has none of the associations which it carries in normal usage. This is an example of a not uncommon situation where a term may be positively misleading, may fail to convey the truth which it is meant to convey. 'Transubstantiation' fails to convey to many the change which has taken place, a real change which is the necessary condition for the spiritual action of Christ in and through the consecrated elements, an action in which, nevertheless, they all believe.

On the other hand, there is something less than plausible in Cranmer's argumentation against the 'real' presence, when, relying on St. Augustine, he continues 'how the sacraments of Christ's flesh and blood be called His flesh and blood, and yet indeed they be not His flesh and blood, but the sacraments thereof, signifying unto the godly receivers that, as they corporally feed of the bread and wine . . . so spiritually they feed of Christ's very flesh and drink of His very blood. And we be in such sort united unto Him that His flesh is made our flesh, His Holy Spirit uniting us and Him so together that we be flesh of His flesh and bone of His bones and make all one mystical body, whereof He is the head and we the members.'

Cranmer is clearly moving here from metaphor to reality and back again in a way which serves only to heighten the incomprehensibility of that which he is trying to clarify. Feeding 'spiritually' on Christ's 'very flesh' is, of course, precisely what all Christians believe. We do not feed 'carnally' on that flesh. When Berengar was required to accept a confession of faith which included the words 'the true body and blood of our Lord . . . are . . . broken and crushed by the teeth of the faithful' he was being asked to confess something which, by implication, was false, suggesting as it did that the teeth of the faithful have any sort of effect on the body of Christ.

Obviously, these are all questions of philosophical terminology, having as much or as little to do with the realities of faith as theories of perception have to do with our appreciation of a work of art. Of course, we have to try to express what we believe, what we are doing, in human language. But, unless we are sufficiently aware of the limitations of that language, it can betray the truth even whilst it claims to express it.

(iii)

A good example of the way in which we can become prisoners of our imagination and of imaginative language is provided by the difficulty which Cranmer had in acknowledging what we call the Real Presence. Since Christ's body is 'really' in heaven how can it be equally 'really' present on the altar? The simple answer is, of course, that it is precisely because Christ's body is now 'glorified', is, as we say, 'in heaven', and therefore freed from the limitations of time and space that He can be so present throughout the world, really though sacramentally. Not that Christ's body is multiplied a millionfold, any more than the omnipresence of God means that He is extended throughout the universe. This is the way we may picture Him. But the truth is that He is neither very large nor very small. The terms simply do not apply to spiritual realities, still less to God. The soul of a six-foot man is not twice as large as the soul of a small child, nor is the love of a mother divided up between her children, in the sense that, if she has five children, each of them gets approximately a fifth of her affection. She may have only a limited amount of time or energy to devote to each; but all the time, at least in the ideal situation, she is loving them all, fully.

These are some examples of the way in which our language, conditioned as it is by our space-time experience, cannot be applied directly to realities that are not so conditioned. When, at the Last Supper, Jesus instituted the Holy Eucharist, He was, as we say, anticipating the situation which would not arise, 'historically', until He had risen from the dead. Even during the forty days before His ascension, He manifested, within a space-time world, some of the independence of space and time which He now enjoyed. In His eucharistic, sacramental life, He can be really present in the totality of His being, human and divine, therefore in a true sense corporeal, because to us human beings His bodily presence has, ever since the Incarnation, been the vehicle for His spiritual action. To emphasise the spiritual activity of Christ at the expense of His real presence, is to undervalue the Incarnation; to emphasise the presence at the expense of the spiritual activity is to do an even greater disservice to the loving work of Christ. Although he used unnecessarily

63

violent language, there is more than a grain of truth in Cranmer's condemnation of the dangers implicit in the doctrine of transubstantiation.

'The final end of all this antichrist's doctrine is none other, but by subtilty and craft, to bring Christian people from the true honouring of Christ unto the greatest idolatry that ever was.' He was concerned that 'devotion to the Blessed Sacrament' was, in fact and in practice, at least distracting people from a direct awareness of the spiritual work of Christ in the world and in the souls of men. Manifestly, true devotion can be an effective means to a deepening of our sense of Christ's love, to an enrichment of our personal relationship with Him, to a strengthening of the bonds of unity between ourselves and our fellow-Christians, who share with us in the eucharistic fellowship, in the banquet to which we are all invited. Cranmer's words may serve to recall us to a more balanced and a more fruitful attitude to Christ's great gift of Himself in the eucharistic species. But no service is done, either to truth or to Christian love, by intemperate language. In the quest for fuller understanding we must all proceed with cautious humility.

(iv)

It is in this spirit that we must approach the other aspect of eucharistic doctrine which has divided Western Christendom even more than the nature of Christ's sacramental presence, namely the question of the relationship between the Lord's Supper, the service of Holy Communion, the Mass (as it is variously called) and the atoning death of Jesus on the Cross. And here it will be helpful to recall the background to much of the debate that went on during the sixteenth century both in this country and on the continent. The more one studies the history of the Reformation and of the events that led up to it, the clearer it becomes that the whole movement was motivated much more by political and even social factors than by any purely theological dissatisfaction. After all, theological debate had been a recurrent feature of Christian history from a very early age. But it is only when cultural, political and nationalistic factors come in that permanent divisions become established, the supreme example being the great schism between the Greek East and the Latin West. It must surely be so, since persecution, mutual intolerance and even outright war are incompatible with an authentic Christian devotion to the truth that must ever be combined with love.

The way in which the Western Church had developed led to two serious causes of spiritual impoverishment and, as it was felt, betrayal of the authentic spirit of Christ. The confusion of the temporal power of the Papacy with the spiritual jurisdiction of the Bishop of Rome was one major reason why, when revolt broke out against papal authority, the princes of the West, far from throwing their support behind the Pope, were only too glad to take the opportunity of rejecting some of the claims which they regarded as unjustified and extravagant. The sack of Rome by the troops of the king of France in 1527 occurred several years before Henry VIII's decision to renounce the authority of the Vicar of Christ.

In Germany, the Princes were only too anxious to extend their power and wealth at the expense of the great ecclesiastical landowners, whilst the peasants in their turn rebelled against the nobles, one of the many manifestations of rising social unrest, seen in our own country in such incidents as Wat Tyler's rebellion and Jack Cade's attack on Canterbury and Lambeth. Wyclif's association with John of Gaunt in his anti-papal policies was another indication of a growing dissatisfaction with the attempt of the Church's central bureaucracy to control the entire social and political spectrum of human life. It was widely felt that the institutional Church had lost much of its spiritual authority because its own spiritual ideals had been grossly tarnished. One of the German princes who remained loyal to the Church could nevertheless write as follows:

E

'If the Roman Church were to lose 10,000 ducats of her revenues, excommunications would be hurled and swords drawn and all Christians called upon for aid; but if 100,000 souls through the fraud of the devil are brought to ruin, the Chief Shepherd unites himself to the councils of him who is continually bent on injuring and enslaving Christendom.'

The attack on 'the Church' was, essentially, an attack on the clergy, both higher and lower, who had come to be seen as usurping a position and playing a role which reduced the laity to an inferior and unprivileged position. It was Wyclif who made the first explicit condemnation of this attitude:

'When people speak of holy Church they understand thereby prelates and priests, monks and canons and friars, and all men that have crowns [sc. are tonsured], though they live never so cursedly against God's law, and call not nor hold secular men to be of holy Church, though they live never so faithfully after God's law and die in perfect charity.'

It is in the light of this conviction that we can best understand the objection of the Reformers to anything that tended to underline the separateness of the clergy and the corresponding degradation of the laity. It was, for example, the underlying reason for the demand that the chalice should be restored to the laity, as it was for the insistence on the 'priesthood of the laity', which was to be one of the most emphatic assertions of reformers of every shade of opinion.

In the context of our present concern, it was this above all which sparked off the attack on the prevailing eucharistic doctrine and practice. For the Mass had come to be seen as the prerogative of the ordained minister, who was seen as controlling and manipulating the treasures of Christ's redeeming work. Thus Cranmer could say:

'If we put the oblation of the priest *in the stead of the oblation* of Christ, refusing to receive the sacrament of

His body and blood ourselves, as He ordained, and trusting to have remission of our sins by the sacrifice of the priest in the mass . . . we do not only injury to Christ but also commit most detestable idolatry. For these be but false doctrines, without shame devised and feigned by wicked popish priests, idolators, monks and friars which *for lucre* have altered and corrupted the most holy supper of the Lord and turned it into manifest idolatry . . .

And forasmuch as in such masses is manifest wickedness and idolatry, wherein *the priest alone* maketh oblation satisfactory, and applieth the same for the quick and the dead *at his will and pleasure,* all such popish masses are to be clearly taken away out of Christian churches and the true use of the Lord's supper is to be restored again; wherein godly people assembled together may receive the sacrament every man for himself, to declare that he remembereth what benefit he had received by the death of Christ, and to testify that he is a member of Christ's body, fed with His flesh and drinking His blood spiritually.'

The words emphasised in the foregoing passage make it clear that Cranmer's chief objection to current Roman practice was based on the view that the priest alone controlled and applied the sacrificial work of Christ 'at his will and pleasure' irrespective of the state of mind of the individual. That there might well be abuses connected with the priestly prerogative, we can hardly doubt. Certainly Cranmer believed that the development of daily private masses, unknown in the early Church as they were (are are) still unknown in the Orthodox Church

'sprang up of late years, partly through the ignorance and superstitition of unlearned monks and friars, which knew not what a sacrifice was but made of the mass a sacrifice propitiatory, to remit both sin and the pain due for the same; but chiefly they sprang of lucre and gain, when priests found the means to sell masses to the people which caused masses so much to increase that every day was said an infinite number . . . '

(v)

It is here then that we come to the crucial issue. How are we to understand the relationship between the celebration by the Church of the eucharistic liturgy (whether we call it Holy Communion, Lord's Supper, Mass or, simply, the Eucharist) and the sacrificial death of Christ on the Cross. We all acknowledge that there is some sort of relationship. On the one hand, the Catholic view is that the sacrifice of the altar is, in some sense, the same reality as the sacrifice of the Cross. On the other hand, as we know, many within the Reformed tradition insist that it is a mere reminder, commemoration, memorial of that saving event. It is the contention of the following argument that, paradoxical as it must be thought, *both are right*. The Mass or the Eucharist is, in an important sense, no more than a memorial of Calvary. Equally, in an even more important sense, it is identical with Calvary. Nor is this just a piece of sophistry, an ingenious but disingenuous way of surmounting an impasse.

Let us begin by making it clear what the orthodox Catholic position does not teach. It does not mean or imply that the events of Calvary—the nailing of Christ to the Cross, the draining away of His life-blood, the final agony and death are in any sense renewed or repeated. Christ died once and once only. His death is the once for all historical event, unrepeated, unrepeatable, whereby He redeems the world That death is unrepeatable precisely because it is an event of human history, like the death of the two men who were crucified along with Him, like the betrayal of Judas, the denial of Peter, the hand-washing of Pilate. All these things belong to history. History does not in the strict sense repeat itself.

When, therefore, the Reformers argued that Christ's death is simply commemorated in the eucharist, they were absolutely right, in so far as they were refusing to admit that Christ can be put to death again, that the historical events which we think of as the Passion and Death of Christ can be re-enacted. These events of course re-presented, as the Passion play of Oberammergau in some sense re-presents, the story of the Passion. But this is not what the eucharist does. It is not a dramatic re-enactment of past events, events that are over and done with. 'We know that Christ once raised from the dead does not die any more' (Rom. 6: 9). Whatever the Church does in her eucharistic celebrations, she is certainly not repeating the events of Calvary. She is recalling them to mind.

She is recalling them to mind because of their underlying significance. For, as we have already thought, the events of Calvary are of abiding significance because they are the outward expression of an inner reality. That inner reality is precisely the essential sacrifice of Christ. For, once again, we must remind ourselves that it was not what Christ did or suffered which, in itself, was of redemptive value. The redemption was achieved indeed through the suffering and the death because these were the manifestation, the outward expression, the visible embodiment of that attitude of obedience which, as we have seen, gave its value to whatever Christ experienced. The essence of Christ's sacrifice is the invisible, intangible, abiding act of Christ's human will, an abiding fact, ever present to the Father, but rendered visible as a matter of historical fact in the events of Christ's human experience. It is in this sense that we can talk of the Lamb 'slain in sacrifice ever since the world was established' (Rev. 13: 8). It is in this sense that we must understand the words 'the priesthood which Jesus holds is perpetual, since he remains for ever' (Heb. 7: 24).

If we may so express it, from God's point of view Calvary was no more than incidental to the sacrifice of His Son; things might have turned out differently, yet the obedience of Christ, the essence of His sacrificial attitude would have been just the same; the world would have been redeemed. But for us human beings Calvary is of supreme importance because it is on Calvary that we are allowed to see Christ's obedience working itself out. And here a passage from the Council of Trent is profoundly relevant.

'He then, our Lord and God, was on the point of offering himself, by His death on the altar of the Cross, once and for all to the Father, in order thereby to bring about our eternal redemption; yet His priesthood was not to be terminated with His death (Heb. 7 : 24, 27). So, at the last supper, on the night of His betrayal, in order that He might leave to His beloved spouse the Church a sacrifice which can be seen (*sacrificium visibile*) to meet the needs of human nature, a sacrifice in which that sacrifice of blood-letting to be carried out once for all on the cross might be represented (*repraesentaretur*) and the memory of it (*eiusque memoria*) might endure to the end of time and its saving power might be applied for the remitting of the sins we daily commit; showing that He was constituted a "priest for ever in the line of Melchisedech", He offered up to God the Father His body and blood under the appearances of bread and wine and under the signs (*symbolis*) of these realities gave them to His apostles. . . .'

This was promulgated on 17 September, 1562. It is interesting to compare with them some words which Cranmer had written some thirteen years earlier:

'Although in a certain kind of speech we may say that every day we make a sacrifice of Christ, yet in very deed to speak properly we make no sacrifice of Him but only a commemoration and remembrance of that sacrifice which He alone made and never none but He.'

He also quotes with approval the words of Peter Lombard:

'That which is offered and consecrated of the priest is called a sacrifice and oblation because it is a *memory* and *representation* of the true sacrifice and holy oblation made on the altar of the cross.'

And finally

'In this eating and drinking and using of the Lord's supper, we make not of Christ a new sacrifice propitiatory for remission of sin.'

Now, obviously what Cranmer was concerned to do was almost precisely what Trent was to do, to emphasise the unique and unrepeatable nature of Christ's redemptive sacrifice. He was concerned about the sort of language which might seem to diminish the supreme and absolute value of the Cross. For example:

'If they make every day the same oblation and sacrifice for sin that Christ himself made, and the oblation was His death . . . then followeth it of necessity that they every day slay Christ and shed His blood'.

Cranmer was not just being perverse. He was clearly motivated by a genuine desire to safeguard the authentic tradition against what he saw to be deviations from it. Dr. Francis Clark has tried to show that there is no substantial evidence to suggest that pre-Reformation Catholicism was not completely orthodox in this respect. All one can say is that, even today, language is still used which would imply that the Mass derives its efficacy from the fact that it is a 'renewal' of Calvary. Thus, a missal in general use talks about 're-enacting' the sufferings of Christ. A popular 'handbook of the Catholic faith' says: 'The actual natural separation of Body and Soul is *renewed* and made *present* under the symbols of bread and wine'. A similar publication declares: 'Every day throughout the world the sacrifice of Christ is *renewed*'. We know, of course, that the authors do not really mean what they are saying. The point is that they are saying

71

it. They can hardly call the Cranmerian kettle black when the pot is so suspiciously subfusc.

(vi)

The disagreement between 'Roman' and 'Reformed' doctrine about the eucharist (omitting all the non-theological factors already referred to) derives very largely from the fact that two levels of reality are here involved and the antagonists are not always aware of this fact. At one level the Mass is, can be, no more than a memorial, a looking back, a bearing-in-mind of certain events that took place on a hill near Jerusalem on a certain April day in (probably) A.D. 33. These events were the externalisation, the rendering visible of an internal, invisible power, the sacrificial, obediential love of Jesus. Those present on Calvary, even if they could hardly have been aware of it at the time, were witnessing the sacrifice of our redemption, because they were seeing the *outward manifestation* of that sacrifice. Only the eye of God could witness the reality.

Christ's purpose in instituting the eucharist was to make it possible for His followers, to the end of time, wherever they might find themselves, to witness *the same sacrifice,* manifested outwardly in a totally different form. What happened on Calvary was that, for the first time in human history, something took place which enabled men to be present, to witness, to take part, if they so willed, in the self-offering of Christ ('I lay down my life of my own free will'). Wherever and whenever the eucharistic sacrifice is enacted, men are enabled to be just as truly present, to witness, to share in the sacrificial work of the redeemer. It is not that 'Calvary', that is to say the events which took place on the hill of Calvary on that distant day are brought into the twentieth century, rather we in the twentieth (or any other) century are brought into the presence of Christ-dying-risen-glorified who, because He is 'in heaven', is no longer bound by the conditions of our space-time world and can be equally present wherever and whenever His followers are met together.

But why, it will be asked, is Calvary not sufficient? Why have the eucharist at all? In one sense, of course, Calvary is all-sufficient, in the sense that Christ's redeeming of us is a once-for-all achievement. 'As one man's fall brought condemnation so the good act of one man brings everyone life' (Rom. 5: 18). But it is equally true to say that the work of redemption is an ongoing process, since it will not be finally realised until the last soul is gathered in. This is the Church's mission, the work of every Christian to enable the grace of Christ to be brought to generation after generation of mankind. And here again we may see how Cranmer was struggling towards this sort of idea.

> 'The controversy is not whether in the Holy Communion be made a sacrifice or not . . . but whether it be a propitiatory sacrifice or not and whether only the priest make the said sacrifice. . . .'

The problem for him was made acute by the picture of the active, 'sacrificing' priest and the totally passive laity, on whose behalf the sacrifice was being made. His instinct was right. He felt that the laity must also be actively involved in whatever was taking place.

> ·   'It is the sacrifice of all Christian people to remember Christ's death, to laud and thank Him for it, and to publish and shew it abroad unto others for His honour and glory.'

It is, in fact, much more than that. It is the 'sacrifice of all Christian people' precisely because we are all invited to share in Christ's sacrificial activity, not simply by allowing His sacrifice to bear fruit in us by our passive acquiescence, but by our active self-surrender through the sort of sacrificial obedience whereby we have been redeemed. 'I dedicate myself for their sakes, so that they in turn may be dedicated through the truth' (John 17: 19). 'If we have become incorporate with him in a death like his, we shall also be one with him in a resurrection like his' (Rom. 6: 5). Christ's sacrifice is something in which we are actively involved. He has instituted the holy eucharist as both a memorial of His own redemptive work and a present reality by means of which we are directly and immediately associated with Him in that work.

In the words of the Holy Communion service:

> 'We offer and present unto thee, O Lord, ourselves, our souls and bodies, to be a reasonable, holy and lively sacrifice unto thee; humbly beseeching thee that all we who are partakers of this holy communion may be fulfilled with thy grace and heavenly benediction. And although we be unworthy, through our manifold sins, to offer unto thee any sacrifice, yet we beseech thee to accept this our bounden duty and service. . . .'

In the Roman Mass the priest speaks of 'my sacrifice which is also yours', which means much more than the suffering of the divine Victim. It implies an association of the community with Christ in a total sacrificial act. So, in the traditional prayer which has, unfortunately, been much truncated in the reformed rites:

> 'O God, whose marvellous work established our human nature in its worthiness and, in a still more marvellous work, refashioned it: grant us through the mystery of this water and wine to become sharers of His divine nature who willed to share in our human nature, even Jesus Christ your son, our Lord. . . .'

Both traditions then recognise that what is happening at the altar is no mere reminder of a past event. It is an energising, enriching, sanctifying, present activity. This, in the end, is what matters—the growing together in holiness of life and mutual love of the whole body of the faithful. Debates about the mechanics of the process, about the precise nature of the relationship of altar to cross, are justifiable, are indeed tolerable only if they somehow enable us to enter more fully, heart and mind, into the marvellous work of our redemption. For that redemption, we must remember, although it is essentially the work of Christ our Lord, nevertheless demands our co-operation if it is to be made effective. In the words of Augustine: 'God created you without your compliance; He will not save you without it'. (*Deus te creavit sine te: non te salvabit sine te.*) For salvation and sanctification are not achieved by a passive inactivity; they are brought about by a wholehearted response to the offered grace. That grace was indeed won for us on Calvary; but it is made effective here and now through the continuing active presence of Christ in His Church, specifically in His sacramental activity, above all through that self-giving in the eucharist, a self-giving which invites a self-giving on our part.

> 'You did not choose me; I chose you. The task I have appointed for you is that you should go out and bear fruit. . . . If a man lives on in me and I in him, then he will yield abundant fruit; separated from me you are powerless to do anything. . . . I have bestowed my love upon you, just as my Father has bestowed his love upon me; live on then in my love. You will live on in my love, if you keep my commandments, just as it is by keeping his commandments that I live on in his love' (John 15: 16, 5, 9–10).

The whole process of our redemption, of Christ's work in and for us brings up again and again the same point. Human nature, created for a life of happiness in obedience to God's will, is disfigured by the sin that is obedience. It is restored to its integrity in the individual human nature of Christ, through the obedience which finally brought Him to the Cross. 'Glorified' by the Father, He is for ever freed from the limiting conditions of our mortality, conditions to which we remain subjected. Yet, through the eucharist, He has made it possible for us to reach out to Him, to touch Him, to receive the living reality that He is, living in His flesh which, ever since the incarnation, is the vehicle of the divine life. Admittedly, by itself, 'the flesh is of no avail'. But the flesh of Christ is indissolubly united with His spirit, that human spirit which, in its turn, is indissolubly united with the divinity. Through Him, then, human nature is enabled to be united with the divine nature, the 'image and likeness of God' restored. The very availability of Christ's selfhood in the eucharist is at once a stimulus and an effective empowerment.

In both the Roman and the Anglican forms of eucharistic worship the great hymn of Christ's triumph reaches its climax in the wonderful outburst

> 'By whom and with whom in the unity of the Holy Spirit all honour and glory be unto thee, O Father Almighty, world without end'.

Or, in the slightly fuller Roman form,

> 'Through him, with him, in him in the unity of the Holy Spirit all honour and glory is yours, Almighty Father, for ever and ever'.

In face of that stupendous proclamation our shabby disagreements about how and when and what are shown up for the squalid trivialities that they are.

CHAPTER VI

HEALING THE BROKEN BODY

'Just as this loaf was scattered all over the mountains and
having been brought together was made one, so let your
Church be gathered from the ends of the earth in your kingdom.' Didache 9 : 4.

'Once upon a time men took into your temple the first
fruits of their harvests, the flower of their flocks. But the
offering you really want, the offering you mysteriously need
every day to appease your hunger, to slake your thirst, is
nothing less than the growth of the world. . . .This bread,
our toil, is of itself, I know, but an immense fragmentation;
this wine, our pain, is no more, I know, than a draught that
dissolves. Yet in the very depths of this formless mass you
have implanted . . . a desire, irresistible, hallowing, which
makes us, believer and unbeliever alike, cry out, "Lord, make
us one".' Teilhard de Chardin, *Hymn of the Universe*, p. 20.

(i)

A well-known rejection of 'Roman' eucharistic teaching is to
be found in Article XXXI, which runs as follows:

> 'The offering of Christ once made is the perfect
> redemption, propitiation and satisfaction for all the
> sins of the whole world, both original and actual, and
> there is none other satisfaction for sin but that alone.
> Wherefore the sacrifices of Masses in the which it was
> commonly said that the priests did offer Christ for the
> quick and the dead, to have remission of pain or guilt,
> were blasphemous fables, and dangerous deceits.'

The substance of this article dates from 1553, some nine years before the Council of Trent in which, as we have seen, it was solemnly defined that Christ's death on the altar of the Cross is a 'once and for all' offering which brought about 'our eternal redemption'. In other words, the article is aimed not at official Catholic doctrine but at perversions of it.

Corresponding to this rejection of what is alleged to be Catholic teaching is, of course, the condemnation of Anglican Orders in the Bull *Apostolicae Curae* of 1893. The basic ground on which this document declared those Orders 'absolutely null and utterly void' was, apparently, the view that, since in the sixteenth century the Church of England rejected the notion of a sacrificing priesthood, there was a complete absence of that correct intention, expressed in due form, which is necessary for a valid ordination. But again we have seen reasons to suppose that, in denying the teaching that the Mass is truly a sacrifice, the sixteenth century Protestants were rejecting the idea which (mistakenly) they attributed to Catholics, namely that the Mass is, so to say, a sacrifice altogether in its own right, something which the priest claimed to be able to offer by his own power, *pro libidine suo*, at his own whim. The division arose and was to a great extent perpetuated because such an idea was seen as introducing within the Body of Christ, which is the Church, a division into two sections, the active, officiating, controlling clergy, and the passive, receptive, manipulated laity.

In the words of Cranmer, in his Defence of the True Catholic Doctrine about the Sacrament of the Body and Blood of Christ:

> '*Omnes memoriam mortis Christi celebrant, omnes Deo gratias agunt, omnes ad poenitentiam et mutationem vitae feruntur, omnes se quasi sacrificium Deo offerunt, omnes illum pro Deo et Servatore habent, omnes illum spiritualiter epulantur, cujus rei certissimum argumentum perceptionem panis et vini in coena faciunt.*
> All celebrate the memorial of Christ's death, all give

thanks to God, all are moved to penance and amend-
ment of life, all offer themselves to God in a kind of
sacrifice, all take Him for their God and Saviour, all
feed on Him spiritually; the surest guarantee of all this
is made by them in receiving the bread and wine at the
supper.'

It is worth while comparing this passage from Cranmer
with a document which was promulgated in Rome in 1967.
Entitled 'An Instruction on the Worship of the Eucharistic
Mystery' issued by the Sacred Congregation of Rites, it contains the following significant, even striking, words:

'It should be made clear that all who gather for the
Eucharist constitute that holy people which, together
with the ministers, plays its part in the sacred action. It
is indeed the priest alone who, acting in the person of
Christ, consecrates the bread and wine; the role of the
faithful in the Eucharist is to recall the passion, resurrection and glorification of the Lord, to give thanks to
God, and to offer the immaculate victim not only
through the hands of the priest but also together with
him; and finally by receiving the Body of the Lord to
perfect that communion with God and among themselves which should be the product of participation in
the sacrifice of the Mass.'

It seems not unreasonable to suggest that, had such a statement been available in the sixteenth century, the differences
between the Roman Church and the Reformers would have
been considerably narrowed.

The dogmatic theologian will seek to emend Cranmer's
pronouncement in detail. The ordinary Christian will surely
see it as an inspiring and encouraging call to find in Holy
Communion an authentic means of grace through his union
with Christ present in the sacramental species. And if we are
at one at this point, it is by this same means that we shall find
the patience, the humility, the tolerance, the sympathetic

understanding of another point of view, above all the true Christian love which can pursue the truth without acrimony, without seeking to score points, without fear of losing face.

In the light of all this, what are the prospects for an ever closer drawing together until we achieve something like the condition of the primitive Church when 'the whole body of believers was united in heart and soul' (Acts 4: 32)? Such a unity cannot be imposed from above. It is something that must grow within the general body of the faithful. This means that every individual Christian has a personal responsibility for rebuilding the unity of the Body of Christ which has been fragmented by our quarrels and disagreements, not least, alas, over that very reality which was instituted by Him to draw us closer to Him and therefore closer to one another.

Now if this is true, if the Eucharist is the supreme means for deepening within us that authentic life in the Spirit which is the condition for our growth in Christian understanding and Christian sensibility, it follows that our failure to achieve a common mind springs in no small measure from a lack of true appreciation of the inner meaning of this great gift. True as it may be that the very intensity of the debate that has gone on down the centuries on this very subject indicates the depth of concern which believers have felt about it, the bitterness with which the debate has all too often been conducted shows a sad failure to grasp the essential nature of that which is under discussion. A married couple may quarrel about many things. If they begin to quarrel about their love, they can only be encouraged to stop and ask themselves what they understand by love.

(ii)

Above all, then, in this time of Lent when we remind ourselves that Christ offered himself to redeem the whole of mankind, we must examine ourselves and our attitude to our fellow-men. Do I, as I approach the table of the Lord's Supper, truly remember that I am uniting myself with the undying power of One who died that all men might live, who rose again to show us that that life reaches beyond the narrow confines of birth and death, beyond the limiting factors of time and space? Do I genuinely seek to lift up my heart, to rise above the trivialities of my anxious concerns, my petty quarrels, my bruised feelings, my earthly ambitions? Even if the Holy Eucharist were no more than a reminder of Calvary, it would still shame us, as we compared our achievement with His, our cowardice with His courage, our selfcentredness with His boundless compassion.

But if it is also, as we believe, the sign and manifestation of the ever-present sacrificial love of Jesus, the abiding self-giving which is the goal and fulfilment of all genuine love, if we really do 'feed' on Him, why is it that we remain ourselves so unloving, or so limited in our love, so unready to give? The answer is to be sought in a lack of that faith which Jesus himself demands if He is to be able to work in us effectively, to fill us with His life-giving Spirit. 'Whoever sees the Son and believes in him shall have eternal life' (John 6: 40). Faith *in Him* is the pre-condition for His being able to effect in us that which His presence implies, means, is.

Once again, we need to try to get behind the philosophical and theological speculations about this faith to the underlying reality which the experts are seeking to describe, conceptualise and define. The living reality that our faith is (or should be) necessarily eludes the categories of the metaphysician or the semantic practitioner as the love between two human beings is so much more than the descriptions of it given by the psychologist, the moralist or even the poet. For faith, which we all too often think of as an intellectual assent to a set of propositions, is essentially a relationship of my whole personality to the person and the being of Christ. It obviously implies a certain intellectual content, just as a loving relationship between two human beings is a 'marriage of true minds'. But love is so much more than this. It is an all-pervading force which conditions all the lover's thoughts,

F

attitudes, concerns, hopes, activities, desires. When, for example, the poet asks

> How do I love thee?

and answers the question thus

> I love thee to the depth and breadth and height
> My soul can reach, when feeling out of sight
> For the ends of Being and ideal Grace.
> I love thee to the level of every day's
> Most quiet need, by sun and candle light . . .

she is far from attempting to define or even to describe love. Yet she is communicating a reality, even if that reality can be recognised only by those who have shared her experience.

It is scarcely a coincidence that Paul writes in the same sort of way about the Christian's relationship to Christ.

> 'May you be strong to grasp . . . what is the length and breadth and height and depth of the love of Christ, and to know it, though it is beyond knowledge. So may you attain to fullness of being the fullness of God himself.'

For faith in Christ is inseparable from the love of Him, from a loving response to His own communicated love. Indeed, Paul has just been praying 'that through faith Christ may dwell in your hearts in love' (Eph. 3: 17–18). Nor is he writing to a community of mystics. As the last two chapters of the same letter make clear, he is writing to the ordinary Christian, beset with the problems and even the temptations of life in a pagan world. But he sees the power of Christ as a force that can overcome every kind of division, even what had been the greatest division of them all.

> 'Gentiles and Jews, he has made the two one, and in his own body of flesh and blood has broken down the enmity which stood like a dividing wall between them; for he annulled the law with its rules and regulations so as to create out of the two a single new humanity in

himself, thereby making peace. This was his purpose, to reconcile the two in a single body to God, through the cross, on which he killed the enmity' (Eph. 2 : 14–16).

(iii)

We know, of course, that to a certain extent Paul was speaking of an ideal situation. Some years before the letter to the Ephesians was written, he had had occasion to upbraid the Corinthians for the divisions existing in their community. The point is that Paul sees in the body and blood of Christ a power which is able to reconcile all men, whatever their enmity. Writing as he was in what we may call the afterglow of the historical events of Christ's death and resurrection, his words may have been expected to make a stronger impact than they perhaps do today when the remoteness of those temporal happenings may evoke in us a weakened response.

Yet it has been the argument of much of this book that the purpose of the institution of the eucharist by Jesus was precisely to effect a present, historical, visible reality which should be not less truly a manifestation of His saving sacrifice than was His actual death of the Cross. Indeed it is not unfair to argue that the saving power of Jesus was less obviously manifested in the shame and suffering of Calvary than it is in the sacramental activity of the altar. For at least, however we describe or define that sacramental activity, we are undeniably in the presence of some procedure which has a religious significance. Had we been present on Calvary, what should we have discerned in all that squalor and degradation, that heartbreaking pain, that torn and bleeding body but a cruel judicial murder? We at least have behind us nineteen centuries during which Christians have meditated on those events, have speculated about their significance, have learnt to see in them the work of our redemption. And if the first generation of Christians had the testimony of those who had seen the Risen Lord, we have the abiding witness of the Church to perpetuate and strengthen that testimony.

We have no excuse. The message of the cross, the message of the resurrection, the message of Paul, the ever-growing message of the Church constitute a body of argument which ought to be irresistible.

> 'With all these witnesses to faith around us like a cloud, we must throw off every encumbrance, every sin to which we cling, and run with resolution the race for which we are entered, our eyes fixed on Jesus, on whom faith depends from start to finish. Jesus, who, for the sake of the joy that lay ahead of him, endured the cross, making light of its disgrace' (Heb. 12: 1-2).

'Our eyes fixed on Jesus.' Here is the clue. We have failed to keep our eyes fixed on Him, preferring to fix our eyes on some particular interpreter of His teaching, Aquinas or Luther, Zwingli or Wesley, or any of a score of theologians of various schools. These may be helpful in giving a new insight into that teaching. But it is the teaching or, rather, the active presence of Christ which is what matters. As a recent writer has pointed out, speculation about the Real Presence tends to substitute the question 'What is present?' for the real question 'Who is present?' Some sort of doctrinal affirmation may be necessary in a community of believers, in order to help preserve unity. But the reality in which, in whom we believe eludes definition. Certainly, if the definition becomes no more than a shibboleth to which we cling for its own sake, this is not to do any service to the truth. Rather is it to inhibit growth in our appreciation of the underlying truth. As Coleridge put it:

> 'The maxim contains past knowledge and is retrospective, and the idea contains future knowledge and is prospective.'

In the same way, the dogmatic definition may be a useful summary of past approaches to a theological idea; it may help to point the way forward to a deeper appreciation of that idea. But the idea will best communicate itself through our personal desire to understand it and to make it a life-giving force in our whole experience.

(iv)

If this is true of theological teaching in general, it is especially true of the matter with which we are here concerned. Perhaps the most powerful factor which has inhibited our complete unselfconscious surrender to Jesus in His eucharistic presence is the fact that all the metaphysical discussion about the Real Presence, all the probing into the relationship between the Eucharist as a present reality and the Cross as a past event, all the sectarian debate about a mystery which essentially transcends our divisions has made us, as indivual Christians, too cerebral in our approach to the simple yet marvellous actuality of Christ coming to us, in all His power, under the veils of bread and wine. In the presence of that actuality, metaphysical expertise is valueless compared with the unquestioning acceptance of the unlettered, unsophisticated believer who, receiving the consecrated host, has no doubt that he is indeed receiving the fullness of the powerful presence of the Incarnate Word. He seeks for, he needs no 'explanation', any more than the lover, vouchsafed the gift of love, thinks of interpreting it in the light of Freudian psychology or bodily chemistry. In so far as he adverts to these related but peripheral factors, to that extent will he be distracted from the central reality.

C. S. Lewis, as always, has wise things to say on this topic:

'I could wish that no definitions had even been felt to be necessary; and still more that none had been allowed to make divisions between the churches. . . . However it may be to others, for me the something which holds together and "informs" all the objects, words, and actions of this rite is unknown and unimaginable. I am not saying to any one in the world: "Your explanation is wrong". I am saying: "Your explanation leaves the mystery for me still a mystery". Yet I find no difficulty in believing that the veil between the worlds, nowhere else (for me) so opaque to the intellect, is nowhere else so thin and permeable to divine operation. Here a hand from the hidden country touches not only my soul but my body. Here the prig, the don, the modern, in me have no privilege over the savage or the child' (*Letters to Malcolm,* p. 133).

It is not until we stop trying to *understand,* that we shall arrive at the point where the unimpeded action of Christ has its full effect in us.

When the day comes on which Christians of every denomination think primarily, if not exclusively, of the simple fact that the same Lord is working in us, when we stop discussing and allow Him to act, then will the unifying power of the eucharist begin to make itself felt. Theological analysis and joint discussions are desirable and indeed inevitable in a situation where the various institutional churches must do all they can to break down the very barriers which they themselves have erected. For that reason we must welcome the 'agreed statement' on eucharistic doctrine in which the international commission set up by the Anglican and Roman Catholic authorities proclaims the basis of our common faith.

'When His people are gathered at the eucharist to commemorate His saving acts for our redemption, Christ makes effective among us the eternal benefits of His victory and elicits and renews our response of faith, thanksgiving and self surrender. Christ through the Holy Spirit in the Eucharist builds up the life of the Church, strengthens its fellowship and furthers its mission. The identity of the Church as the body of Christ is both expressed and effectively proclaimed by its being centred in, and partaking of, His body and blood. In the whole action of the Eucharist and in and by His sacramental presence given through bread and wine, the crucified and risen Lord, according to His promise, offers himself to His people.'

Here surely is the heart of the matter, the essential core of all that it is necessary to believe in order that we may participate fruitfully and dynamically in the life-giving work of our common Lord. It is through the individual's reception of the sacraments (even within a communal act of worship) that the Church itself is enriched by the grace of God. It is important always to bear in mind that the institutional church is the means; the sanctification of the individual Christian is the end. To quote C. S. Lewis once more:

> 'In every Church, in every institution, there is something which sooner or later works against the very purpose for which it came into existence' (ibid., p. 63).

The institutional Church will, therefore, be enabled to do its work more effectively, the more the individual members of it are concerned chiefly with the affair of their personal and corporate sanctification and less with the outward prosperity or efficient functioning of the ecclesiastical machine. The Church is there to help its members on their way to God. In the measure in which it fails in that purpose, in that measure has it failed to be true to itself.

(v)

In the light of these considerations, something must be said here about a question which is increasingly presenting itself to those who take seriously the ecumenical vocation which they have accepted, the question of a common sharing of the table of their common Lord. Eight years and more have now passed since the Vatican Council's Decree on Ecumenism, *Unitatis Redintegratio,* contained this hopeful passage:

'It is unlawful to regard shared worship (*communicatio in sacris*) as a means to be employed *without discretion* for the restoration of Christian unity. Such worship is based on two principles: to express the unity of the Church and to be a sharing in the means of grace. *As a general rule,* the fact that it expresses unity forbids it. The grace to be obtained by it *from time to time* recommends it. In practice, it is left to the prudent decision of the local bishop, exercising his authority with due regard to the circumstances of the occasion, the locality and the individuals involved, unless the Bishops' conference or the Holy See should decide otherwise.

The words emphasised indicate that there can be exceptions to the general rule. The interpretation of the passage by local hierarchies (following the Directory) has been so restrictive as in practice to close the door which thus seemed to be opening. It is a well-known fact that there are occasions of ecumenical meetings for prayer and the study of matters of common concern where the members are satisfied that the measure of unity achieved is already such as to justify a departure from the 'general rule'; the experience of the 'grace obtained' is a further assurance that they are acting entirely in accordance with the spirit of the Decree, however much that spirit may have been stifled by the letter of subsequent legislation. It is not easy to see how they can be regarded as disloyal to the Church which, under the guidance of the Spirit in the Council, was moved to proclaim this beginning of a greater liberty. It would seem to be truer to suggest that the disloyalty is theirs who have set their faces against any such development.

What, we may ask, is the measure of unity that is required if we are to be permitted to give expression to it in a shared act of eucharistic worship? Clearly, unless we are to become hopelessly legalistic in our approach to this most interior and spiritual of all matters, we cannot assess 'unity' simply in terms of a purely formal, external, structural togetherness. The unity for which Christ prayed was, is, a unity in a shared love of Him and of one another. However necessary, in practice, it may be to institute some Test Act or Act of Uniformity for administrative and other similar purposes, no Christian worthy of the name can subscribe to the view that this is the only guarantee of authentic unity. Again and again we must resist the temptation to substitute for Christ's own valuation some purely conventional criterion of acceptability. 'This is the test by which men will know that you are disciples of mine, if you have love one for another' (John 13: 35). Nor are mere verbal expressions of faith sufficient. 'Not everyone who addresses me "Lord, Lord" will qualify for the kingdom . . . ' (Matt. 7: 21).

Who then is to find fault with those who, convinced that their unity in the love of Jesus is as complete as it is likely to be in this world, seek to give expression to that love in a sharing of that which is both a token of existing love and a means of intensifying it. And to those who dismiss this as mere sentiment, it is enough to ask: 'Since when has a worthy sentiment been anything but an inspiration to noble deeds?' The appeal of Oxfam and of a hundred good causes is an appeal to the head (and the purse) through the heart. It is a denial of the richness of the Christian life to suggest that emotion is to be disregarded, treated with a suspicion, denied its authentic expression. Saint John, as we know, introduces the story of the Last Supper with the words: 'He had always loved those in the world who were his own; he loved them to the end' (John 13: 1).

Discretion, as the Vatican Council decreed, must be observed. But discretion is not synonymous with inactivity, still less with cowardice. Those who have the courage of their Christian convictions may well be making a greater contribution to Christian unity than those who are for ever counselling caution, declaring that the time is not yet ripe, suiting their pace to the least enthusiastic—least enthusiastic because least concerned.

Nor should this be construed as a plea for indiscriminate opening of altars to all and sundry, regardless of sincere conviction or theological soundness. In the nature of things the occasions under discussion are likely to be rare enough, and certainly untypical of the life of the Church at large. Yet the way forward would seem to lie through a recognition of the witness that such people are bearing to the reality of faith, the resolution of hope, the vigour of charity exemplified in their conduct.

Admittedly there are problems. Authority has the right and indeed the duty to control any activities which might threaten the unity of the Roman Catholic Church which is, as the Vatican Council proclaimed, the paradigm of all Christian unity. But the fact that certain extravagant and potentially disruptive experiments and practices are not infrequently associated with indiscriminate inter-communion does not logically entail the condemnation of any invitation to communion extended to our separated brethren, in circumstances very different from the behaviour of extremists. It is the extremists on either wing who impair the Church's unity, not those moderates who believe that a living reality such as the Church is, must manifest signs of life and growth if it is to be true to itself.

Underlying what we may call this secondary debate is, of course, the deeper question of the validity of Anglican Orders. In a book of this kind, there is little to be said about that problem save this. Important as it is to safeguard as far as humanly possible the correctness of the procedures which have been authorised by the Church to perpetuate the precious gift of Christ's sacramental presence, there is an ever-present danger of supposing that God himself is necessarily bound by those same procedures. What this means can be best elucidated by commenting on a sentence from a speech delivered by Cardinal Vaughan ten days after the promulgation of *Apostolicae Curae:*

'How shocking to adore as very God elements that are

but bread and wine, and to bend down after auricular confession to receive a mere human and useless absolution!'

Now, even supposing that the condemnation of Anglican Orders was historically justified and theologically substantiated, it seems curiously unchristian to allege that there is anything 'shocking' in the conduct of those who, in good faith, even if mistakenly, are adoring God, thought to be present in the elements. For, of course, the adoration is directed to God, not to the elements as such. If a Roman Catholic priest were, for whatever reason, to consecrate 'invalidly' would his conduct and that of his congregation be 'shocking' if they were 'to adore as very God elements that are but bread and wine'?

Again, it is to take a very mechanical view of sacramental absolution to allege that the prayer of the 'invalidly' ordained priest is merely 'human' and therefore 'useless'. Does the sorrow of the penitent and the faith of the priest count for nothing with God?

(vi)

We may, then, conclude our study of this our common Christian concern with the prayerful hope that the wealth of faith and love which, down the centuries, has been directed to Christ in His sacramental presence (however that presence be envisaged), will be seen and accepted by God in the spirit of humble worship in which it has been offered. Those who hold fast to the simple basic truth that the test of our Christian conviction is the strength and endurance of our Christian love, will not easily surrender to the spirit of recrimination which has disfigured so much debate about the precious reality of Christ's sacramental presence.

At the beginning of our investigation into this saving mystery we pictured Jesus in the Upper Room with His friends. Perhaps we should end by calling to mind some of the prayers that they recited together on that night when they recalled the bounteous generosity of God, His abiding power, His redeeming work. Although the prayers are taken from a modern version of the Passover there is no reason to doubt that substantially they go back to the time of our Lord.

> Blessed art thou, O Lord our God, King of the universe, who didst choose us from all peoples to proclaim thy unity throughout the world and to sanctify our lives by observing thy commandments. In thy love thou hast given us, O Lord our God, holy days for gladness, festivals and sacred seasons for rejoicing, even this feast of unleavened bread, the season of our freedom, whereon we worship thee and remember the Exodus from Egypt.

> How manifold are the favours which God has bestowed on us. . . .
> He has commanded us to establish His kingdom throughout the world, so that all men may form a single band to do His will with a perfect heart. Blessed art thou, O Lord, redeemer of Israel and of all mankind.
> May God in His mercy permit us to witness the days of the Messiah and to inherit everlasting life.
> He who makes peace in His high places, may He grant peace to us and to all Israel, and let us say Amen.
> I shall not die but live, and declare the works of the Lord.